Understanding Capital

Understanding Capital
Marx's Economic Theory

Duncan K. Foley

Harvard University Press
Cambridge, Massachusetts, and London, England   1986

Library of Congress Cataloging-in-Publication Data

Foley, Duncan K.
   Understanding capital.

   Bibliography: p.
   Includes index.
   1. Capital.   2. Marx, Karl, 1818–1883.   Das Kapital.
3. Marxian economics.   I. Title.
HB501.F644   1986   335.4′1   86-4736
ISBN 0-674-92087-2 (alk. paper)
ISBN 0-674-92088-0 (pbk.: alk. paper)

To my students
with thanks for all they have taught me

Preface

This book is intended to be a guide to fundamental passages in Marx's writings on economics and to the overall structure of Marx's economic ideas. I have provided references to pertinent chapters of *Capital* because I believe that anyone who is seriously interested in learning what Marx thought about economics must go beyond reading a guide of this kind to reading what Marx wrote. At the end of the book, I have made suggestions for further reading, choosing those references that are helpful either because they are very clearly written or because they exemplify a particular point of view. A more complete bibliography can be found in the *Dictionary of Marxist Thought* (Bottomore et al., 1984).

I have used mathematics to illustrate and explain the theory in some places. The level of mathematics is about the same as that demanded by an intermediate-level undergraduate economic theory course.

My aim is to provide a general introduction to Marx's economic theory rather than to argue for a particular interpretation. But the reader should know that I take a controversial and unconventional stand on the treatment of prices and labor values, the value of labor-power, and what I call the value of money and unequal exchange. Serious scholars of Marxist theory whose opinion I respect have criticized my explanation of these topics and have questioned my choice of vocabulary in discussing them. I believe that my treatment of these topics is faithful to Marx's conception. But even more important, I believe that this way of approaching the problem has decisive pedagogical advantages. The interpretation I rely on offers a simple, direct, and transparent explanation of the relation between the labor theory of value and the phenomenal world of money and prices. It avoids the pitfall of imposing a very complex discussion of levels of abstraction on the student first encountering the labor theory of value. A student who has grasped my interpretation will be in a good position to understand the arguments for other interpretations as well.

Among the many people who have helped me understand Marxist economics, I would particularly like to acknowledge Michael and Susan Carter, Jens Christiansen, Jack Gurley, Donald Harris, Bridget O'Laughlin, Chiranjib and Gita Sen, Alexander Thompson, Robert Williams, and the other participants in the political economy seminar at Stanford University during my time there and Suzanne de Brunhoff, Gerard Dumenil, Laurence Harris, David Levine, Dominique Levy, Alain Lipietz, John Roemer, Jesse Schwartz, Anwar Shaikh, Edward Wolff, and the students in my course in Marxist economic theory at Barnard College of Columbia University.

Alice Amsden, Andre Burgstaller, Gerard Dumenil, Donald Harris, Stephen Marglin, Deborah Milenkovitch, Lance Taylor, and Edward Wolff have given me helpful comments on the drafts of this book. Michael Aronson of Harvard University Press offered me important encouragement and support at a critical point in this project. Jodi Simpson's work on my manuscript has resulted in innumerable improvements in force and clarity.

Quotations from *Grundrisse: Foundations of the Critique of Political Economy* by Karl Marx, translated by Martin Nicolaus (Harmondsworth and New York: Penguin Books and Random House; copyright 1973, Martin Nicolaus) are reprinted by permission of the publishers. Quotations from the following books are reprinted by permission of International Publishers Company: *Capital*, Volumes 1, 2, and 3, by Karl Marx, edited by F. Engels (copyright 1967); *Theories of Surplus Value* by Karl Marx (copyright 1963); *A Contribution to the Critique of Political Economy* by Karl Marx, edited by Maurice Dobb (copyright 1970); *Selected Works* by Karl Marx and Frederick Engels (copyright 1968).

Finally I would like to thank my wife, Helene Peet Foley, for bearing in many ways the most burdensome costs of my pursuit of this path, and my son, Nicholas, who somehow manages to give me back more energy than he uses up.

Contents

Understanding Capital

1

On Reading Marx: Method

Marx's philosophical and methodological presumptions are unfamiliar to many readers, and this unfamiliarity leads to unnecessary misreadings of Marx, especially to failures to locate his statements properly in terms of level of abstraction and connection to earlier texts. In this chapter I shall point out a few important characteristics of Marx's way of thinking and writing in an attempt to forestall such misreadings.

A Historical and Changing Reality

Marx conceives of the social reality he is analyzing as a process that evolves in response to its own internal contradictions. In other words, the phenomena he discusses cannot be understood independently of the history that produced them. This approach contrasts with the view that phenomena will tend to reassert themselves regardless of historical context. He sees the relations he is studying as being in a constant process of change, not just unchanging elements undergoing some rearrangement. Thus Marx's aim is not to state universal principles that explain human and social interaction once and for all but to understand the regularities that govern the changes in specific social formations. In fact, those features of human life that do appear to be universal and can be attributed to "human nature" or to the existential situation of human beings are of secondary interest to Marx. He tries to find those aspects of a social situation that uniquely identify it and make it specific in historical terms. In the introduction to the *Grundrisse,* Marx (1939, p. 85) makes this point explicitly in relation to the category of production:

> [Some] determinations will be shared by the most modern epoch and the most ancient. No production will be thinkable without them; however, even though the most developed languages have laws and characteristics in common with the least developed, nevertheless, just those things which determine their development, i.e. the elements which are not general and common, must be separated out from the determinations valid for production as such, so that in their unity . . . their essential difference is not forgotten. The whole profundity of those modern economists who demonstrate the eternity and harmoniousness of the existing social relations lies in this forgetting.

The Human Production of Knowledge

The knowledge people have of social reality is, for Marx, a human product and has no existence outside the activity of living human beings. Knowledge is a cumulative social creation, like a human city, and has many aspects of its production and reproduction: teaching, maintenance, critical correction, wholesale destruction and replacement, opening of new territories, and so on. In particular Marx does not think that knowledge exists somewhere "out there" in the mind of God or in a preexisting library and that human activity simply uncovers it. Human activity creates knowledge in the way that it creates art or products. This activity is social, in that every producer of knowledge begins with knowledge inherited from the past and works in a context of human beings reproducing and altering this knowledge in their own ways.

For Marx no production of knowledge occurs without active intervention in the world. People find out about the world by trying to change or control it (or, at the least, by trying to uncover its secrets through systematic observation), not by a process of abstract speculation. This view of knowledge as historical and changing entails a central role for the method of criticism—the sifting, questioning, and correcting of existing knowledge. Marx in this sense is not particularly interested in being "original." He wants to find the kernel of truth in the knowledge constructed by others. His criticism in this sense is positive—despite the sometimes scornful tone he adopts—in that he believes there is some truth, at some level, in every systematic expression of ideas and the problem is to discover what that truth and its level are.

Thus we must carefully distinguish between instances in which Marx is reporting or reworking ideas he receives from other thinkers and those in which he is proposing a corrected formulation. This care is especially important around central economic problems: the theory of value, which Marx takes largely from Ricardo and Ricardo's correction of Smith; the distinction between productive and unproductive labor, which Marx takes from Smith and gives a historical significance; and the theory of the tendency for the rate of profit to fall in capitalist economies, which Marx views as an accepted discovery of the classical economists and seeks to explain rationally within the context of his understanding of the dynamics of capitalist production.

There are important similarities of form between knowledge and reality in Marx's way of thinking. But it is important to recognize that he never identifies the two, neither along the Hegelian line of seeing reality as the product of thought itself nor along the empiricist line of seeing knowledge as a simple, unmediated reflection of reality.

The Structure of Knowledge

Marx adopts a great part of Hegel's analysis of the structure of human knowledge, a form he views as constant even though its substance is always changing. The basic elements of this structure are what Marx calls *abstractions* or *determinations*, ways of talking about aspects of reality that are separated from and purified of their relations to the whole complex of factors that make up the concrete instance. This idea of abstraction is common in the social sciences, although the specific abstractions that are viewed as relevant, and their status, differ greatly among various theoretical traditions. For example, Marx views "value," "labor," "money," and "commodity" as fundamental abstractions that are vital for understanding the historical specificity of capitalist production; and neoclassical economics sees "tastes," "technology," "resources," and the "market" as fundamental abstractions that are useful in understanding resource allocation in any human society.

The Layering of Determinations

Marx insists on the layering or ordering of abstractions or determinations in theory. For him knowledge is an analyzed mental construct made up of fundamental abstractions or determinations. These abstractions are developed and stated in a particular order and combined to reproduce important features of the real phenomenon in thought. He explains this process very clearly in the introduction to the *Grundrisse* (1939, pp. 100–101):

> It seems to be correct to begin with the real and the concrete, with the real precondition, thus to begin, in economics, with e.g. the population, which is the foundation and the subject of the entire social act of production. However, on closer examination this proves false . . . if I were to begin with the population, this would be a chaotic conception of the whole, and I would then, by means of further determination, move analytically towards ever more simple concepts, from the imagined concrete towards ever thinner abstractions until I had arrived at the simplest determinations. From there the journey would have to be retraced until I had finally arrived at the population again, but this time not as the chaotic conception of the whole, but as a rich totality of many determinations and relations . . . The concrete is concrete because it is the concentration of many determinations, hence unity of the diverse . . . Along the first path the full conception was evaporated to yield an abstract determination; along the second, the abstract determinations lead towards a reproduction of the concrete by way of thought.

This double motion is pervasive in Marx's writing. Thus *Capital* can be seen as a movement to reconstruct in thought the whole complex of capitalist social relations beginning from the simplest abstractions—commodity, value, and money—and eventually arriving at the most complex and distorted forms, for example, the stock market and crisis.

Importance of the Starting Point

Because Marx insists on the ordering of determinations, the starting point of an analysis becomes crucial in establishing the meaning of a theory. The same determinations may appear in very different theories with very different significance because they have a different relation to the whole structure of abstraction. For example, the idea that capitalist competition tends to equalize the rate of profit on capitals engaged in different lines of production appears in essentially the same abstract form in neoclassical and Marxist economic theory, but the significance given to this tendency is quite different in the two theories. In Marxist theory this tendency is an example of the deviation of the money price of commodities from their labor values, as we shall see in Chapter 6, and is an important part of the redistribution of surplus value through exchange relations; in neoclassical theory the equalization of the rate of profit is the core of the idea of efficiency in the allocation of resources achieved by competitive markets.

Modification of Fundamental Determinations by Later Ones

The recreation of a concrete phenomenon by invoking the layered determinations of theory in Marx's thought creates two potentially confusing effects. First, the addition of higher order determinations may produce phenomena that appear to contradict the fundamental determinations. For example, the higher order determination that the equalization of the rate of profit through redistribution of surplus value in exchange obscures the fundamental determinations that labor produces value and that surplus value corresponds to unpaid labor because in the higher order determination the surplus value appropriated by an individual firm may not correspond to the labor exploited by it. But this type of contradiction is only apparent; as long as the explanation is consistent with the structure of the theory, the fundamental determinations continue to be valid and important in the explanation and continue to operate in the more complex situation. This can be seen if the higher order determinations are removed and the fundamental ones allowed to operate without qualification. We do not view the fact that buildings do not fall to the ground as a contradiction of the law of gravity because it is precisely the law of gravity that allows us to understand why the physical properties of beams can hold the building up and because if those physical properties are altered the law of gravity does reassert itself in the collapse of the building.

The fundamental determinations often show themselves in the aggregate or average behavior of a system. Thus the origin of surplus value in unpaid labor may not be very apparent when we look at one capitalist firm, but it becomes much clearer when we look at the ensemble of all the capitalist firms. Fundamental principles often appear in the form of conservation principles that apply to a whole system. The labor theory of value appears at the level of the whole system of commodity production to be such a conservation law—value is produced by labor and conserved in exchange. This principle implies that the factors governing the production of value are quite different from those governing its distribution. Marx often fails to be explicit about the level of aggregation at which he is working. He frequently explains the aggregate behavior of a system by discussing a typical or average element of it. For instance, in the first three chapters of *Capital* he discusses the laws that apply to a typical, or average, commodity. These laws in fact apply to the aggregate of all social production and are unlikely to apply to any particular real individual commodity, which carries with it many peculiar higher level determinations. Likewise, in the whole first volume of *Capital* Marx talks about an average or typical capital, which is in fact the aggregate capital, or a scale model of the aggregate capital.

Self-Determination and Tautology

For Marx the abstractions that constitute a theory define each other. It is impossible to understand one of these abstractions outside the system comprising all of them. The idea of value, for instance, will turn out to comprise many aspects, including exchange value, money, and abstract labor. When we ask what value is, Marx will say it is the form labor takes in a commodity-producing society. When we ask what abstract labor is, Marx answers that it is the aspect of labor in a commodity-producing society that produces value. Thus the whole cluster of ideas concerning value constitute a self-determined system. This strikes some people as circular and tautological, a mere abstract spinning out of logical categories. Indeed, Marx himself comments on the dangers of an excessively "Hegelian" mode of presentation of his theory, in which the structure of ideas seems to construct itself.

It is important to realize that there is nothing illegitimate or irrelevant about Marx's way of thinking. The theory can be tested: the articulation of the concepts developed must be coherent and logical and the development must not be arbitrary or *ad hoc*. Even a well-constructed theory must pass a further test, namely, that its self-determined articulation actually corresponds to and illuminates some class of real phenomena. Marx can demonstrate logically (or dialectically) that in "commodity production" the relations of value, exchange value, and labor necessarily take a certain form. Nevertheless, we still have to be convinced that the society we want to study (probably our own) is in fact an instance of "commodity production," or "capitalist production." If the explanations we get out of Marx's theory seem strained or wrong or unhelpful, we would be justified in arguing that we are not in fact dealing with commodity production as Marx envisions it. The theory becomes tautological only if we begin to invoke *ad hoc* principles to save the fundamental determinations in the face of real anomalies.

In fact, all theories, including those of the physical sciences, have this self-determined character. In Newtonian mechanics, for example, the definitions of the concepts of force and mass are inextricably interdependent. The most important scientific statements about the world are neither tautologies nor statements of empirical fact but helpful theoretical relations that are self-determined and at the same time illuminate a fundamental relation in the world.

Explanation through the Ordering of Determinations

The basic activity of science lies in the explanation of phenomena. In Marx's terms a good explanation consists in locating the phenomenon in relation to the ordered set of determinations the theory proposes in such a way that the phenomenon is reproduced by the combination of the determinations of the theory while the most fundamental determinations continue to operate. Thus Marx's explanation of capitalist production and the origin of surplus value requires not only that the principles of the general theory of commodity and of value continue to hold in capitalist production but also that the appearance of a surplus value be accounted for. His explanation of interest and the interest rate must take as its basis the whole structure of the theory of capitalist production and surplus value and show how the interest rate emerges from the pressure of the development of capitalist profit-seeking.

Explanation, Determination, and Predetermination

When we see a concrete phenomenon, from Marx's point of view we ought to be able to explain it, that is, show its relation to an ordered structure of abstractions. In this sense Marx believes that reality is *determined*, that is, after-the-fact explicable in terms of a scientific theory. Furthermore, the fundamental abstractions of a theory, if they are correct, must continue to operate as long as the phenomenon in question retains its essential character. Marx sometimes refers to this necessity as "inevitability." It is important to recognize that neither of these positions, nor both taken together, implies that the concrete future is *predetermined*. After something has happened, all its determinations have in fact occurred and we have a chance of figuring out exactly what they all were (or enough of them to feel we understand what went on). But in the future we have no way of knowing all of the determinations that will be active, even if we do believe that we know *some* of them. Thus what actually happens must "inevitably" obey certain basic principles (whether they are principles discovered by physical or social science, for example, the law of gravity or the law of value). Such knowledge is of great use but does not enable us to predict the future and does not mean that the future is predetermined.

Laws and Tendencies

Marx uses the terms *law* and *tendency* to refer to the fundamental determinations of a theory. Thus the *law of value* refers to the necessary relations between value, labor, and money and to the conservation principles that arise from these relations. The *tendency for the rate of profit to fall* in capitalist economies, to take another example, is a reflection of the development of productive forces and technical knowledge through capital accumulation. From what we have already understood about Marx's thought, it is clear that we should not expect laws to be empirically confirmed in every concrete instance (for example, that every successive measurement of the average rate of profit should be smaller than the last one) because there may be intervening determinations of a higher order that qualify or even reverse the tendency at the lower level. This does not mean that the underlying tendency is absent or negated by the higher level determination because the higher level determination has to cope with or work through the lower level tendency. If a car has a tendency to swerve to the right when the driver brakes, this tendency is not erased when the driver compensates for it by steering left while braking. The car may seem to go straight as it slows down, but the tendency to swerve is still apparent to the driver in the effort he makes to compensate for it. In the same way, even if the tendency for the rate of profit to fall is offset, say, by the appropriation of surplus value from colonial possessions or neocolonial clients, the significance of the basic law is unchanged.

No Democracy of Determinations

In neoclassical economic theory the determinations that underlie a situation are usually thought of as operating simultaneously; that is, all the determinations are considered to be equally important in producing the final result. An example of this approach can be found in the neoclassical model of general competitive equilibrium. According to this model there is complete symmetry among all the simultaneous market-clearing conditions that define the competitive equilibrium. This way of thinking is foreign to Marx, who always approaches problems by working out a first approximation corresponding to the simplest or most basic determination and then modifying that solution.

Marx's approach is most striking in his treatment of the transformation problem—the problem of reconciling the labor theory of value with the principle of equalization of rates of profit among different sectors in capitalist production. Whereas modern treatments of this problem invariably approach it through the method of solving simultaneous equations, Marx simply analyzes the first-order consequences of trying to equalize the rate of profit without taking into account the feedback of the change in prices on the valuation of capital. Similarly, in Marx's treatment of the tendency for the rate of profit to fall, he identifies the possibilities that a rise in the rate of exploitation or a cheapening of elements of constant capital may retard a fall in the rate of profit due to the rise in the technical composition of capital as *countertendencies*. But some modern writers view these effects as two simultaneous aspects of the process of technical progress under capitalism.

Marx sometimes ends his analysis (especially in sections of *Capital* that he never finished) with the study of the first approximation and does not systematically introduce the higher layers of determination. Still, the transparency of the results he obtains by insisting on the ordering of determinations—in contrast to the inevitably ambiguous results of simultaneous methods—is a great scientific advantage.

Models and Theories

A word is in order on the problem of models and examples in Marx's work. As we have seen, Marx views theory as a complex and ordered structure of abstractions constructed as a way of knowing the world. Theory is itself a contradictory entity because any theory contains within itself the seeds of its own transformation, latent inconsistencies whose development will open the way to new understandings. A model, on the other hand, is a representation of a theory in which these contradictory elements have been suppressed, often to allow a mathematical representation of the ideas. Models are representations not of reality but of a theory. Each theory can generate a large number of models, each of which could claim to represent some aspect of the theory but none of which is identical with the theory. In fact, no model can be identical with the theory it represents precisely because it suppresses contradictions that have a real life in the theory. This approach also contrasts sharply with the methodological practice of neoclassical economics, where the main effort is in the investigation of the properties of abstract models and a central role is played by the problem of the relation of the model to reality.

Dialectics

The dialectical element in Marx's thinking and writing appears in two ways. First, Marx always strives to bring to the surface the dialectical process of critical transformation of ideas that is characteristic of all fertile theoretical work. Whereas many theoretical writers hide the process by which they arrive at their concepts—a process that surely involves the dialectical reworking of existing concepts—Marx brings this process into the foreground of his writing. For example, instead of simply stating the results of his thinking about the theory of money, Marx tries to reproduce the dialectical movement that carries us from the concept of the commodity to the concept of money. This is primarily a matter of style and presentation.

The second, deeper, effect of the dialectic in Marx's work lies in his understanding of the nature of reality and the nature of knowledge. Marx's vision of a reality that is a contradictory process of change rather than a static arrangement of preexisting entities exerts the most profound dialectical influences on his thought. Similarly, Marx accepts as a matter of fact the idea that human knowledge, as a human construct, has these same characteristics of motion and change. These characteristics of Marx's thought are disconcerting and disorienting to those who see knowledge as a collection of truths that never change once they have been discovered or revealed.

2

The Commodity:
Labor, Value, Money

Systems of Production

All human societies produce to meet their material needs. In some societies products come into being as the property of particular agents who exchange these products through a process of bargaining. The key element in exchange is the practical control over the product held by the agents, who can refuse to part with it unless their terms are met by other agents. Marx calls products that exist in such a system of ownership and exchange *commodities*, and he begins *Capital* with a discussion of them. The theory of the commodity form of production provides a way of investigating certain aspects of systems of production organized by exchange.

Systems of production that do not have exchange relations at all or exhibit them only marginally are not commodity-producing systems. Many noncapitalist societies produce the bulk of their material needs entirely within household units—through hunting, gathering, and basic agriculture—and distribute these products entirely on the basis of household or family relationships or in accord with custom. Marx believed that among the Incas in Peru all products became the property of the king and were centralized under royal control and redistributed directly by the central regime. In theory, in a socialist or communist society products come into being as the property of the whole society (perhaps formally as the property of the State) and are distributed according to rules and policies established on a social level. In all these cases we can clearly see both production and distribution, but exchange of privately owned products is not the way distribution is accomplished.

Even in a commodity-producing society, an important part of production does not take a commodity form. Indeed, subsistence and household production play a major role in highly developed commodity systems. The preparation of a family meal and the maintenance of a family automobile by its owner are clearly products that go to meet material needs, but these products are not exchanged for other products and therefore do not take the form of commodities.

The Dual Nature of Commodities   *(Capital 1.1.1)*

In a commodity-producing society the owner of a product can satisfy her material needs in two ways. She can directly consume the product, or she can meet her need indirectly by exchanging the product for another product to consume. Thus the commodity has two aspects: it is directly useful to someone, or in Adam Smith's words, which Marx takes over, it is a *use-value;* and it can also be exchanged for other commodities. This characteristic of exchangeability Marx calls *value.** It is important to understand that Marx views value as a substance that is contained in definite quantities in every commodity produced in a commodity-producing society. This substance is socially determined because it arises from the fact that the commodity is a product in a system of production organized through exchange. Every commodity contains a certain amount of value, and the mass of all commodities newly produced in a society in a period of time also contains a certain value, the aggregate *value added* of all the newly produced commodities.

As we shall see in more detail in the next section, Marx argues that *money* is an expression of this value that is separated from any particular commodity. The money value added of the mass of newly produced commodities is a measure of the total value contained in them. When we move forward from the value that is contained in commodities, we get to money.

As we shall also see in more detail, Marx accepts the view consolidated by Ricardo that what produces value in commodities is

* References to passages in Marx's *Capital* are in the form 1.1 or 1.1.3; the first numeral specifies the number of the volume, the second the chapter, and the third the section within the chapter.

the expenditure of human labor in their production. Thus when we move backward from the value that is contained in commodities we arrive at labor time.

We can summarize the basic structure of Marx's theory as follows: There are special laws that arise in societies in which production is organized through exchange. These laws pertain to the dual nature of exchanged products (or commodities), which have both a use-value, like all useful products in any human society, and a value (or power to be exchanged with other commodities), which is a characteristic unique to commodity production. Value is created by labor and shows itself in the form of money, which is just value separated from any particular commodity.

The Labor Theory of Value

The labor theory of value can be stated simply as the principle that the source of the value added of the mass of commodities produced is the labor expended in producing them. If we count up the total labor time expended in the actual production of commodities, making appropriate adjustments that will be discussed in more detail later, that labor time must be the substance of the total value added contained in the commodities.

The unit of money—say, the dollar—is the way society measures value when it is separated from particular commodities. Hence we can measure the total value added in the society in monetary units. In the United States in the early 1980s, for example, the aggregate national value added was about $3 trillion ($3 \times 10^{12}$). The employed labor force was about 100 million (1×10^8) persons. If these employed persons had worked a standard 40-hour week for 50 weeks of the year (which is not quite right because many persons were employed part time) and if all had been employed in the actual production of commodities (which is not true because much employment, as we shall see later, is devoted to the distribution rather than to the production of values), then the total labor time expended would have been 200,000 million (2×10^{11}) hours. According to the labor theory of value, this labor time and this value added are two different aspects of the same thing. Labor creates value, which is expressed in money terms. In this example, 1 hour of labor contributed $15 of value added.

We can give this equivalence another quantitative meaning by calculating the amount of labor time a dollar represents in a particular period. For the example above, a dollar represents 1/15 hour of social labor (or about 4 minutes). This ratio we shall call the *value of money* because it tells us how much labor time the monetary unit represents. We have noted that for the average situation an hour's labor time produces $15 worth of value added. This relation is the reciprocal of the value of money and is called the *monetary expression of value* because it tells us how much value in monetary units an hour of labor time creates. The value of money will change over time because of changes in the productivity of labor and also because of general changes in the prices of all commodities—inflation or deflation.

The value of money must not be confused with the inverse of the *wage rate*. If the average wage rate is $5 an hour, one can buy 1/5 hour of labor-power (the capacity to perform labor) for a dollar, even though the dollar represents only 1/15 hour of social labor.

The basic idea of the labor theory of value is that the mass of newly produced commodities contains the total productive social labor time and that this value is expressed in terms of money, a form of value that is separate from any particular commodity.

Value-Producing Labor   *(Capital 1.1.2)*

Marx takes the labor theory of value from Ricardo and makes some important critical corrections to his formulation. The most important correction, which runs through Marx's whole discussion, is the location of the labor theory of value at the level of the aggregate production of commodities (or of the average commodity), not, as Ricardo expressed it, in each particular commodity. Marx also refines the labor theory of value by carefully analyzing the concept of labor that is needed to make the labor theory of value consistent. His critical corrections concerning the concept of labor can be summarized in the following statement: the labor that produces value is *abstract* rather than concrete, *simple* rather than compound, *social* rather than private, and *necessary* rather than wasted.

The most difficult of these ideas is the concept of abstract labor. Marx points out that whenever we see someone working we see them doing some specific task as part of some specific production process. We see someone spinning thread or weaving cloth or punching data or smelting iron. All these acts of labor are *concrete* labors, aimed at producing a particular use-value. But, Marx argues, it would be peculiar to say that weaving labor or data-processing labor was *the* labor that produced value, because when we look at a whole commodity-producing society we see that every kind of concrete labor adds value to its product. Marx argues, then, that in a commodity-producing society it is labor in general, or *abstract* labor, that produces value. Another way to understand this point is to see that in a commodity-producing society all types of concrete labor have the capacity to produce value. When we abstract from the concrete peculiarities of specific types of labor, we are left with the common character of production of value.

Marx acknowledges, as Ricardo does, that individuals differ in their capacity to produce value. Whether these differences are innate or the result of different persons having reached different stages of development of their productive powers because of different life experiences is not particularly important in this context. An hour of one person's labor may produce more value than an hour of another's. To cope with this phenomenon within the framework of the labor theory of value, both Marx and Ricardo propose to measure labor time in terms of a basic unit, which Marx calls *simple* labor—the amount of labor expended in an hour by those workers who have no particular advantages of skill or experience in production. The labor of more skilled or experienced workers, which produces more value in an hour, Marx views as being a multiple of simple labor.

Some labor is expended privately in a commodity-producing society. This labor produces use-values just as does the labor expended to produce commodities, and these use-values may be quite essential to the reproduction of the society (think, in particular, of domestic labor in housekeeping and childrearing). But because the products of this private labor are not exchanged on the market, they are not commodities and contain no value in the technical sense. Labor expended privately, then, does not produce value and does not enter directly into the complex social division of labor sustained by the exchange of commodities. Thus Marx argues that only *social* labor—that is, labor devoted to the production of commodities actually exchanged—produces value.

Finally, it is clear that the mere expenditure of labor time does not add to the value of commodities unless that labor time is *necessary* for the production of the commodity at the current level of technical development. Even if someone expends more labor than is necessary for the production of a commodity, the commodity sells for the same price as another produced with less labor time; thus the extra labor produces no value. What regulates the production of value is the amount of labor currently needed to produce the commodities, an amount that is always changing because of technical discoveries and improvements in processes of production and because of exhaustion or discovery of natural resources. Marx makes explicit the point that only labor necessary at the current social level of development of productive technique adds value to the commodity.

These qualifications of the labor theory of value make the theory consistent with the gross features of real commodity production. If we were to try to find operational equivalents for the concepts of the labor theory of value, we would have to devise practical methods to measure abstract, simple, social, and necessary labor time. As is often the case in theoretical–empirical work, many different methods can be proposed to accomplish this. Which method works best in a given context and in the investigation of a particular problem can be discovered only by experimentation and critical evaluation of the results. It is important to realize, however, that the possibility of operationalizing these concepts in several different ways does not mean that they are meaningless or that it is impossible to give them any operational significance. Only if it were impossible to find *any* useful interpretation of these concepts of labor in terms of practically measurable quantities would the labor theory of value lose its scientific interest. It is also important to realize that Marx, in his highly abstract discussion, does not propose any particular method for the measurement of labor time. All he does is to point out the need to make the adjustments we have described.

For example, if we were to study the problem of trade between backward and advanced countries, we would need to establish some equivalence between the labors expended in each country. We cannot simply look at the actual value added created in each country in proportion to labor time because the price system may not accurately reflect relative values (as we shall see in more detail in Chapter 6). But we could try to measure relative labor productivities in a variety of other ways. We could measure the education and training levels characteristic of workers in the two countries. We could also try to match physical productivity measures in those cases in which the same techniques of production were being used in the two places. These techniques could give us some definite idea of how large the gap might be between the value-creating power of labor in the advanced country and in the backward country.

Throughout this book, I shall often use the unqualified word *labor* when the context makes clear that it must mean *abstract, simple, social, and necessary labor time.*

The Money Form of Value   (*Capital* 1.1.3, 1.2)

Once we understand that the value contained in the mass of newly produced commodities is an expression of the abstract aspect of the social, necessary labor expended in their production, we next need to consider how this value is expressed in the form of money. Value is the exchangeability of commodities in Marx's theory. It is a social substance that resides in the commodities and is placed there, so to speak, by the labor expended in their production. Conversely, the ability of commodities to establish a relation of equivalence with each other by changing places through exchange is a reflection of the fact that they all contain the same substance, value. The aim of Marx's theory of money is to show how this value substance must find a social expression as money separate from particular commodities.

Marx's development of this idea begins with the simplest expression of equivalence of two commodities. If 20 yards of linen exchange for one coat, we have the relation

$$20 \text{ yards of linen} = 1 \text{ coat} \tag{2.1}$$

In this expression the order of the commodities makes a considerable difference because we think, in this case, of the coat as measuring or expressing the value of the linen. Marx says that the linen is in the *relative* position and the coat in the *equivalent* position. The coat is a particular equivalent for the linen.

As we shall see later, Marx believes that there are many reasons why particular exchanges in reality will not accurately reflect the quantitative relation between the values of the commodities exchanged. In reality a commodity will often sell above or below its value in relation to other commodities. When developing forms of value we generalize from these disturbances and consider the pure situation in which the two commodities exchanged do have the same value. Or we can think of the linen and the coat as average commodities in the whole system of commodity production, knowing that the average of all commodities must sell at a price that reflects the labor time expended in its production.

Marx analyzes this *elementary form* of the expression of value in the relation between two exchanged commodities in great detail. The core of his discussion is an analogy between the value of commodities and weight, which is inherently quantitative and relative but has no natural absolute scale. We can use one object to measure the weight of another, but the establishment of absolute units of weight or mass is a matter of social convention. In the same way, we can use one valuable commodity to measure the value of another, but the absolute units in which we measure value are a matter of social convention.

The elementary form of value quickly develops into the *expanded form* of value, in which one commodity—say, the linen—is successively equated to the whole range of other commodities, each of them in turn expressing its value. This change corresponds to a change in perspective from an individual exchange to a consideration of the whole system of commodity exchange and a recognition that all the commodities participate in it together. Marx expresses the expanded form of value as an endless series:

$$20 \text{ yards of linen} = 1 \text{ coat or} \qquad (2.2)$$
$$= 10 \text{ pounds of tea or}$$
$$= 1/2 \text{ ton of iron or}$$
$$= \ldots$$

But this expanded form is unstable in a gestalt sense. It is not closed because it can always be expanded by introducing another commodity to the series. It tends to undergo a figure–ground reversal into the *general* form of value, in which one commodity— say, the linen—simultaneously serves as a measure of the value of all the other commodities.

$$\left.\begin{array}{l} 1 \text{ coat} \\ 10 \text{ pounds of tea} \\ 1/2 \text{ ton of iron} \\ 2 \text{ ounces of gold} \\ \ldots \end{array}\right\} = 20 \text{ yards of linen} \qquad (2.3)$$

In this form the linen has become the *general equivalent* measure of the value of all the other commodities. This general equivalent form brings us very close to the money form of value. But at this point any commodity could be put on the right-hand side of (2.3).

For example, the arbitrarily chosen *numeraire* of neoclassical economic theory can also be seen as a general equivalent in Marx's sense.

The final step to the full money form of value is taken when some commodity or some abstract unit of account becomes socially accepted as the general equivalent and is commonly used as the measure of value of commodities. Marx, living in the nineteenth century when the gold standard was the dominant monetary form, assumes that the general equivalent must be a commodity produced, like gold, by human labor. In the twentieth century the evolution of monetary systems has been away from a commodity money system and toward a system in which the general equivalent is an abstract unit of account, like the "dollar," which has a social meaning but no definite equivalent in terms of produced commodities.

The conclusion of this first step in Marx's development of the theory of money is that money arises from the commodity relation itself as an expression of the general exchangeability of commodities separate from any particular commodity. Thus we see how the value contained in the mass of newly produced commodities can express itself in monetary units.

This theory constitutes a powerful criticism of monetary theories that posit a "barter" economy preceding the introduction of money. The barter economies in these theories are in fact fully developed models of commodity production and thus implicitly have all the determinants of the money form of value already. They are barter models only because they have simplified reality by ignoring the money aspect of exchange. Once we understand this, we can see why it becomes very awkward to reintroduce money into these models when it is, in a sense, already there but has been removed by abstraction at the start. The Marxist theory of money also suggests that many real exchanges that appear to be barter transactions are in fact monetary transactions in which the transactors find commodities that have the same monetary value to exchange so that no monetary claim has to change hands to complete the transaction.

Money, Prices, and Value

The whole mass of newly produced commodities contains the whole expenditure of social labor in a particular period of time, and this value expresses itself as the money value added of the mass of commodities. This principle of the labor theory of value enables us to calculate a *value of money*, that is, the average amount of social labor time that it takes to add a dollar's worth of value to commodities.

Each particular commodity in a commodity-producing system has a *price*—the amount of money for which it can be bought or sold. On the one hand the commodity contains a certain amount of labor time, and on the other hand the money represents a certain amount of social labor time. We can see a variety of reasons why there might be a difference between these two quantities. A particular commodity might have a price that represents more or less social labor time than is contained in the commodity. For example, suppose that the raw materials and means of production used up in making a table cost $200 and that the labor time expended in its production was 20 hours. If the value of money is 1/15 hour per dollar, this labor time would be the equivalent of $300. If the price of the table is actually $500, then its price accurately reflects its value. But the price of the table might in fact be $400, or $700, either above or below the value of the table.

The reasons for these differences between price and value in the case of individual commodities lie in the relations between buyers and sellers in the markets on which they are exchanged. The ratios at which commodities actually exchange depend on the bargaining power of the buyers and sellers. If sellers have better information, or monopoly power, or State protection, or if there is a shortage of the commodity, the price will tend to be higher. Symmetrically, if buyers have better information or face severe competition among sellers, or if there is a glut of the commodity, the price will tend to be lower. Thus there is no reason to expect the prices of particular commodities to be proportional to their individual labor values, even under conditions of uniform competition among producers. As we shall see in Chapter 8, Marx identifies a powerful and pervasive force in capitalist production that drives prices away from values for particular commodities, namely, the tendency for profit rates to be equalized in different lines of production by competition among capitals. The profit rate is the ratio of the surplus value in the commodity to the value of the capital tied up in its production. Hence, if different products require different amounts of capital for one unit of labor time, prices must differ from values in order for profit rates to become equal.

We can, from the point of view of the labor theory of value, think of these cases in which prices do not accurately reflect values as cases of *unequal exchange of labor times*, because one party to the transaction receives more value than he or she gives up. When prices do accurately represent values, we say we are dealing with a case of *equal exchange of labor times*, because each transactor receives an exact labor equivalent in the exchange. The terms *equal exchange* and *unequal exchange* in this context refer only to the outcome of the exchange process and only to the movement of labor time between exchangers of commodities. Even when exchangers meet on an exactly equal footing, as competitive capitalist firms are assumed to do, the result may be unequal exchange of labor time equivalents. In this book I shall say "equal exchange" and "unequal exchange," with the understanding that I mean equal (or unequal) exchange of labor times.

Notice that unequal exchange does not violate the principle of the conservation of value in exchange, because what one party gains in value is exactly equal to what the other party loses. The total amount of value is unaffected by the fact that the unequal exchange transfers some of it from one agent to another. There is no inconsistency between the possible existence of unequal exchange and the principle that in the aggregate the value added of all the produced commodities expresses the total labor time expended to produce them. When we aggregate or average over all the commodities produced, the instances of unequal exchange cancel out; and in the aggregate the money value added is an accurate expression of the aggregate social labor time.

Forms of Money and the Value of Money   (Capital 1.3.1)

Once we understand that the money form of value is inherent in commodity relations, we are led to consider the different forms of money, that is, the different social devices that have evolved to perform monetary functions. Marx centers his attention on the problems of systems in which some commodity, such as gold, becomes the general equivalent; such a commodity is called a *money commodity*. When a produced commodity becomes the general equivalent, the monetary unit must be defined as a certain quantity of this money commodity. Marx calls this monetary unit the *standard of price*.

The amount of gold for which any commodity exchanges depends on the relation between the labor time contained in the commodity and the labor time contained in an ounce of gold. Because these labor times are always changing with changes in the technologies of producing commodities and gold, the gold price of commodities will always be in a state of flux.

The amount of gold contained in the standard of price—say, the dollar—is, on the other hand, a matter of social convention, one that (like the regulation of standards of weight and measure) very early comes under the control of the State. In a gold-standard regime the dollar is defined by the State to be, say, 1/20 ounce of gold. To find the dollar price of a commodity we first must find the amount of gold that contains the same amount of labor time as the commodity and then translate that amount of gold into dollars, using the conventionally and legally established relation between the dollar and a certain quantity of gold.

For example, suppose that gold and other commodities exchange at their values (that is, in direct proportion to the amount of labor time contained in them), that an ounce of gold contains 10 hours of labor time, and that a bushel of wheat contains 2 hours of labor. Then 1 ounce of gold will buy 5 bushels of wheat. If the dollar is legally and conventionally defined to be 1/20 ounce of gold, the money price of a bushel of wheat will be $4.

The problem of the determination of the value of money is to a first approximation easily and transparently settled in a commodity money system. The dollar is a certain quantity of gold, which contains a certain amount of labor time, and this definition establishes the relation between the monetary unit, the dollar, and social labor time. (When gold itself sells above or below its value in relation to other commodities because of some intervening factors, this equivalence has to be modified accordingly.) It is important to recognize that this theory of the value of money is incompatible with the quantity of money theory of prices, that is, the idea that the money prices of commodities vary in direct proportion to the quantity of money in existence. For Marx the money prices of commodities vary in inverse proportion to the labor contained in the money commodity and in direct proportion to the labor contained in the particular commodities, regardless of the amount of the money commodity that happens to exist.

In a monetary system in which the general equivalent is an

abstract unit of account, for example, a system in which the dollar has no legally or conventionally defined equivalent in gold, the value of money is determined historically, by the pricing decisions of commodity producers themselves.

Circulation of Money and Hoarding   (Capital 1.3.2.a, 2b, 3a, 3b)

In a commodity money system, how much money is needed to allow the ordinary circulation of commodities? From Marx's point of view the prices of commodities are determined by their conditions of production. Thus the total value of commodities that need to be circulated by money, that is, bought and sold for money, is determined by these production factors and by the amounts of the commodities produced. The amount of money needed to accomplish these transactions in a given period of time depends on how many transactions a typical piece of money—say, a coin—can accomplish in the period—the *velocity of money*. If a coin can participate in an average of 10 transactions in a year (through the agent who receives it in one sale spending it in a purchase) and if the total price of the commodities being circulated is $3 trillion, the system would need $300 million of money to accomplish the circulation. This relation, called the *quantity equation* in traditional economic language, must be drastically modified when we consider systems in which credit plays an important role in financing transactions.

In the quantity of money theory of prices, the quantity equation is used as the basis for the conclusion that the prices of commodities must rise or fall in direct proportion to the amount of money in the economy, through the assumption that the velocity of money and the value of the commodities produced do not change. Marx, in contrast, argues that the quantity equation determines the amount of money necessary to sustain the circulation of commodities. This line of argument then raises the questions, where can the system get more money if the circulation of commodities increases and where does excess money go if the circulation of commodities slackens or the velocity of money rises?

Marx answers these questions by pointing to the existence of *hoards*—stocks of the money commodity that do not circulate. A change in the amount of money the economy needs to circulate commodities can lead to a change in these hoards, releasing or absorbing enough of the money commodity to allow circulation to continue unhindered. This formulation is in sharp contrast to the quantity of money theory of prices, which posits a stable demand for money that would prevent idle stocks of the money commodity from adjusting in this way.

In a monetary system in which there is no money commodity and the general equivalent measure of value is an abstract unit of account, as in late twentieth-century capitalist economies, the problem of adapting means of payment to the needs of circulation is a problem of the expansion and contraction of credit rather than of the expansion and contraction of hoards. Still, Marx's approach to the quantity equation is theoretically important. It suggests that even in a monetary system with an abstract unit of account, that is, in a system in which forms of credit act as means of payment, the correct order of explanation for monetary phenomena runs from the needs of circulation to the mechanisms that meet those needs. This order contrasts with that arising from the quantity theory hypothesis, according to which the needs of circulation adapt to the quantity of money through changes in average money prices.

It is important to realize that in Marx's analysis the determinants of the *value of money* are quite different from the determinants of the *quantity of money*. In a commodity money system the value of money is determined by the labor time required to produce the money commodity and by the standard of price that translates a certain amount of the money commodity into monetary units. The quantity of money is determined by the requirements of circulation through the quantity equation. A larger or smaller quantity of money, in Marx's theory, will have in itself no systematic effect on the value of money.

Paper Money in a Commodity Money System   (Capital 1.3.2c)

Marx uses the general equivalent theory of money to analyze several outstanding problems in monetary theory of the nineteenth century. Some of these, such as the problem of maintaining a full-weight gold coinage in the face of the inevitable wear and tear on coins in circulation, need not detain us. But Marx's treatment of the problem of paper money issued by the State without any guarantee of convertibility into gold at a fixed rate is of considerable interest.

The phenomenon in question arises when the State, usually under the pressure of war finance, begins to print paper money to pay its bills but suspends its promise to redeem this paper in gold at a fixed rate of exchange. The two leading nineteenth-century examples are the issue of paper pounds by the British government during the Napoleonic wars and greenback dollars by the Union during the American Civil War. Marx analyzes these cases, following the arguments of the Banking School of monetary theory, on the assumption that gold continues to function as the general equivalent commodity and to be the standard of price. Thus the gold prices of commodities continue to be regulated by the relative conditions of production of gold and of the commodities, regardless of the issue of paper money by the State. Marx argues that a small issue of paper money can be absorbed by the needs of circulation because agents can re-spend the paper they receive almost immediately. A small issue of paper will circulate at par, that is, the greenback dollar will have the same value as a gold dollar. If the State issues more paper than can be absorbed by circulation, agents will try to get rid of the excess paper money by using it to buy gold. This attempt creates a market for the exchange of paper money and gold and a price in that market, usually called the *discount of paper against gold*. The price of the paper dollar might fall to 50% of the gold dollar, for example, so that it would require two paper dollars to buy the amount of gold contained in the gold dollar. Under these circumstances the prices of commodities in terms of paper money will reflect the discount between the paper money and gold. If the gold price of a bushel of wheat is $4 and the discount of paper against gold is 50%, $8 in paper dollars will buy a bushel of wheat.

In the example above, the excess issue of paper money by the State raises the prices of commodities in terms of paper money through the mechanisms of the discount between paper and gold. This conclusion may appear at first to be the same as that reached by the quantity theory—that an expansion of the money supply forces up the prices of commodities. But there are important differences in the analyses. The quantity theory claims that this effect will occur regardless of whether the expansion in the supply of money is in gold or paper. Furthermore, the quantity theory attributes the rise in commodity prices to excess demand in the market for all commodities as agents try to spend excess money holdings. Marx's analysis applies only to paper money, not to gold; and, in fact, the issue of paper money has no effect on the gold prices of commodities. The mechanism of paper money price changes in Marx's theory has nothing to do with excess demand in the markets for commodities in general because it works through the market in which the paper money exchanges against gold; thus the change in paper money prices are merely a reflection of the discount between paper and gold.

This analysis cannot, however, be the basis of an explanation of the value of money in contemporary monetary systems where there is no money commodity. The essence of Marx's treatment of this problem is that gold continues to function as the general equivalent commodity when the paper money is issued. In contemporary monetary systems there is no comparable money commodity against which paper money can be discounted.

International Monetary Relations   *(Capital 1.3.3c)*

Marx concludes his treatment of money in Volume 1 of *Capital* by showing that the general equivalent theory actually leads to the establishment of a world money once all countries adopt the same commodity as the general equivalent. The labor times of productive workers in different countries are all expressed in terms of a certain quantity of gold, for instance. Thus the money commodity also serves to equalize labor times across national borders and to extend the law of value to the world market.

In contemporary systems in which the value of each country's monetary standard depends on the pricing decisions of commodity producers within that country, there is no comparable single world measure of value. The task of equalizing labor times across national boundaries falls to the international exchange markets, in which the moneys of different countries are traded against each other.

The theory of money is important for the rest of Marx's analysis primarily because it defines the equivalence between money measures of value and labor time. The purpose of Marx's discussion of the theory of money is to show that it is possible to view money as representing labor time and to explain apparent contradictions to this principle. Marx generally assumes that there is a functioning commodity money system and that the labor requirements of the production of the money commodity establish the value of money. Then he translates freely back and forth between money expressions of value and labor time. In this way Marx's theory of money is intended to demystify the appearances of the monetary system.

Things That Have a Price but Contain No Labor   (Capital 1.3.1)

The theory of the commodity and the labor theory of commodity value form a compact and consistent account of basic features of economic relations in commodity-producing societies. But some common features of economic life in such societies at first appear to be in contradiction to the labor theory of value. The most important of such anomalies is the existence of things that are not produced by labor but still have a price. Land is a leading example; the owner of land can appropriate a rent by threatening to exclude other agents from the land, even when the land is totally unimproved by any labor inputs. The positive price of reserves of natural resources (minerals, petroleum, and so on) in the ground, even if they have not been developed in any way, is a special case of land rent in this sense.

The general approach of the labor theory of value to these anomalies is to argue that the origin of value and money forms lies in production and in the commodity form of production. Once money and value forms exist and are developed, agents may transfer value among themselves for reasons other than the buying and selling of commodities. These transfers create no new value; hence they constitute merely a redistribution of the claims on the produced value among the economic agents.

Land rent, from this point of view, arises because the ownership of land gives its owner the power to exclude other agents from the productive use of that land. This power allows the owner of land to bargain with producing agents to secure a certain part of the value added produced, which is the *rent* on the land.

Thus the labor theory of value as developed by Marx suggests that superficially similar phenomena, such as the sale of a produced commodity and the leasing of land, in fact have different theoretical statuses and that different explanatory principles will prove useful in studying them. If we want to understand value relations in commodity production, we should center our attention first of all on conditions of production, on factors such as labor productivity. If we want to understand value relations involving nonproduced things, we should look, not to production, but to the rights involved in ownership of these things and to the bargaining position these rights give their possessors. The value of a commodity reflects something about the real production process of the society, whereas the rent of land reflects primarily the struggle over the distribution of control over the product of social labor.

The Fetishism of Commodities   (Capital 1.1.4)

The commodity form of production imposes a paradoxical consciousness on the human beings who live through it. On the one hand, the commodity form of production is a social form of production because in practice the exchange of products establishes an extensive social division of labor and makes every person highly dependent on a multitude of other people for means of subsistence and means of production. The commodity form creates a vast web of cooperation and interdependence of people. On the other hand, the exchange process creates an illusion of privacy and individual self-reliance; it allows and forces people to construe their existence subjectively as a matter of relations between themselves and things rather than as a matter of relations between themselves and other people. The result is that things are treated as people, and people as things. Commodity relations tend to make people view others instrumentally rather than intersubjectively and to induce people to enter into personal and emotional relations with things.

This curious and pervasive distortion is what Marx means by the *fetishism of commodities*. This idea is the culminating formulation of Marx's lifelong concern with the phenomenon of alienation in modern society. The theory of commodity fetishism allows him to treat alienation as an effect of the specific social relations of commodity-producing societies.

The recognition of commodity fetishism as a pervasive, distorting influence on people's consciousness, however, leads to far-reaching conclusions. It suggests, as Marx himself emphasizes in various places, especially in the *Grundrisse*, that a thorough transformation of social relations will require people to discover social relations of production that transcend the commodity form itself, not just the special distributional consequences of the commodity form that are peculiar to capitalism. For Marx the ultimate aim of revolutionary socialism is the creation of new and workable social relations of production that do not depend on the commodity form and money to mediate people's relation to social production. When we consider how helplessly and deeply dependent we are on commodity forms to meet our needs and mediate our conflicts, we see how radical this view is. Such new social relations would be workable only for people whose characters had changed in essential ways from the personalities typical of highly developed commodity production. In place of the pervasive concern for personal development and personal aggrandizement that motivates commodity producers, there would have to be an instinctive understanding and loyalty to the reproduction of the society in a large sense. People would have to engage routinely in social production, not under the compulsion of threats to their biological or social survival, or under the inducement of bribes of prestige, status, or material comfort, but with a prosaic and transparent understanding that social life requires the performance of social labor. The contradictions between such attitudes and the necessities imposed by the realities of commodity production explain much of the pain and conflict of our epoch. To this Marx offers only the consolation that it is a necessary pain of human growth.

3

The Theory of Capital
and Surplus Value

The Theory of Capital and the Theory of Value

Marx develops the labor theory of value and the theory of the commodity as the conceptual space within which the peculiarities of specifically capitalist production can be studied. Capitalist production as a way of organizing human labor socially through exchange is a special form of commodity production, and it depends on the emergence of the money form of value. The problem now is to see exactly how capitalist production relates to the general form of commodity production.

Capitalist firms operate to make a profit. They sell commodities for more money than they pay for the inputs that produce them. Over the whole system, capitalists thus appropriate a surplus value. Can we explain this on the basis of the labor theory of value?

Circulation of Commodities   *(Capital 1.4)*

When we try to think of the capitalist system of production purely in terms of commodities, we reach several analytical paradoxes. Consider a system of commodity production in which independent producers buy inputs to production, add their own labor to commodities, and sell the commodities for prices that in the aggregate reflect the labor time expended in the value added to the commodities. We could represent the movement of money and commodities in such a system by the diagram:

$$C - M - C' \tag{3.1}$$

where the producer starts with the commodities he has produced (C) and sells them for money (M) as a way of buying another bundle of commodities (C') that better suit his needs. The commodities purchased (C') have the same value as the commodities sold (C). The motive behind this transformation is not any change in the value owned by the producer but the qualitative change in the use-values he consumes.

When we think of the commodity circulation in this way, we realize that the process comes to an end after one round of exchange. Once the producer has exchanged the commodities he initially owns for the bundle he chooses, there is no reason for any further exchange to take place. If the economic process is to continue, the reason for its continuation must be sought outside the process itself, for example, in the external assumption that the next day the producer will once again find himself with commodities C that are not the ones he wants to consume and will be forced to exchange again.

Furthermore, there could be no social surplus value in this system. An individual trader might cleverly manage to buy some commodities below their real values and sell them at or above their real values and in this way appropriate a surplus value through unequal exchange. But whatever these agents gain in surplus value, some other agents must lose, because of the conservation of value in exchange. Producers add value to commodities by expending labor on them, but in general they receive in exchange no more than the equivalent of this labor time. Thus there appears to be no way to explain the pervasive appropriation of surplus value as the basis of economic life within this conception.

Notice also that the only conception of accumulation of value in such a system is for an agent to realize more value by selling commodities than he spends in buying them over a period. The difference must take the form of an accumulation of money by the agent. But this accumulated value is simply withdrawn from commodity circulation through the agent's abstinence from consumption. When the agent finally spends the hoard he has accumulated, he simply returns the money value to circulation and withdraws commodities from circulation of the same value (assuming that the value of money has not changed in the meantime). There is in this conception no systematic process of accumulation.

Capitalist Production   *(Capital 1.4, 1.5)*

Consider, in contrast, capitalist production as we observe it. A capitalist firm begins with value in money form and uses it to buy commodities, which are combined in production to yield a new commodity, one that is sold for more money than the capitalist advanced to begin with. Marx represents this motion in the diagram

$$M - C - M' \tag{3.2a}$$
$$M - C\{MP,LP\} \ldots (P) \ldots C' - M' = M + \Delta M \tag{3.2b}$$

The first form is the simplest form of the capitalist movement of value; it shows the capitalist buying in order to sell and realizing in the sale of commodities more money value than he began with. The second is a more complete description; the commodities bought are inputs to the production process (P), which consists of means of production, MP, and labor-power, LP, and the commodities sold are different, produced commodities, which still sell for more money (the initial outlay, M, and the surplus value ΔM) than the capitalist initially laid out.

This diagram of capitalist circulation corresponds directly to the income, or profit and loss statement, of a capitalist firm:

Sales	$M' = M + \Delta M = C'$	(3.3)
Less costs of inputs	$M = C$	
Equals gross profit	ΔM	

The motive behind the circuit of capital is clearly the fact that M' is bigger than M, that is, that the value at the end of the process is larger than the value at the beginning. The capitalist is in fact indifferent to the particular use-values that are involved in this process because his proximate aim is the surplus value to be gained from the whole cycle.

It is interesting to note, even at this first stage, that the $M - C - M'$ circuit does not reach an ending point but recreates its own initial conditions. The circuit begins with the sum of money M in tension with the possibility of expanding by entering the circuit of capital. The circuit ends with the sum of money M' once again in tension with the possibility of expanding by entering the circuit once more. There is no need to appeal to any external condition to explain why this process repeats itself indefinitely.

The critical questions are where the surplus value in the circuit of capital comes from and how it can be explained within the labor theory of value. Furthermore, it is not enough to explain how individual capitalists might make a surplus value through gaining from unequal exchange. To explain capitalist production as a system of organization of social production, we have to explain how a net social surplus value emerges from this process, a net social surplus value that is not offset by the losses of any group of agents. The commodities the capitalist buys at the outset of the circuit of capital must be, on average, purchased at their values, and the commodities he sells must, on average, be sold at their values.

The only resolution of this puzzle is to suppose that among the commodities the capitalist buys there is one that has the power of creating value as that commodity is used up. If that special commodity's use creates more value than the value of the special commodity itself, that is, if it adds more value to the product than the capitalist had to pay for it, then we have a possible explanation of the origin of a social surplus value. The labor theory of value immediately suggests what this value-creating commodity must be—the capacity of workers to do useful work.

Labor-Power as a Commodity (Capital 1.6)

Marx insists that we must distinguish between *labor-power*—the capacity or potential to do useful labor in production—and *labor* itself—the actual expenditure of human energy with the aim of achieving a productive end. If labor-power were to appear on the market as a commodity and if it were possible to extract more labor from labor-power than the value the capitalist had to pay for the labor-power, then we can understand where the surplus value comes from. This explanation is perfectly consistent with the principles of the labor theory of value, because, in the aggregate, commodities, including labor-power, are bought and sold at their values and value is created only through the expenditure of labor in production.

This analysis enables us to understand exactly what happens between the capitalist and the worker when the capitalist purchases labor-power. The capitalist buys the worker's capacity to do useful labor in exchange for a sum of money, the *wage*, which must in general reflect the value of labor-power. Once this agreement has been reached, the worker has no claim to any part of the product or to any part of its value. The capitalist and the worker do face a further negotiation, however, which concerns the exact conditions under which the capitalist will ask the worker to expend labor: how hard the work will be, at how fast a tempo, how unsafe or toxic the work environment will be, and so on.

It is all very well to show how labor-power has been determined theoretically to explain surplus value in capitalist production. But the appearance of labor-power as a commodity on the market was also a historical event that involved tremendous upheaval and conflict.

Marx explains the *historical* conditions for the appearance of labor-power as a commodity as a twofold liberation of the worker. In the first place the worker must be free to dispose of his or her own labor-power. Thus the worker cannot be bound to a particular labor process, as the serf is in feudal production, or to a particular master, as the slave is in slave production. The emergence of labor-power as a commodity is thus the result of the historical destruction of old and powerful forms of bondage.

But there is another side to the freedom of the worker. A worker will sell her own labor-power to someone else only if she cannot exercise that labor-power on her own behalf. Thus the worker must also be freed in the sense of being denied access to means of production that would allow her to produce a product that she could own and exchange herself. In historical terms this means the appearance of a class of human beings who cannot provide themselves with their own means of production and are forced to sell their labor-power to someone who can provide them with the necessary means of production. The most important aspect of this process has been the displacement of peasants from traditional access to land through enclosures, land reforms, green revolutions, and the like.

The Value of Labor-Power   (*Capital* 1.6, 1.7, 1.9)

The capitalist buys the worker's capacity to labor for a certain sum of money—the wage, or the price of labor-power. As we have seen, money is a form of value; thus we can regard the money paid in wages as the equivalent of a part of the social labor time expended by the society. The *value of labor-power* in this sense is the labor time equivalent of the wage:

$$w^* = mw \tag{3.4}$$

where w^* is the value of labor-power, the number of hours of social labor a worker receives in exchange for an hour of his labor-power; m is the value of money as defined in Chapter 2; and w is the money wage, the amount of money the worker receives for an hour of labor-power. For example, if the wage is $5 per hour and the value of money 1/15 hour per dollar, then the value of labor-power is ($5/hour) $\times$ (1/15 hour /$) = 1/3 hour of social labor time per hour of labor-power.

This equivalence between money wages and the value of labor-power holds in an average or after-the-fact sense. There might be circumstances in which actual wages differed from what we would view as their normal level. In that case it would make sense to say that the value of labor-power equaled the normal level of wages multiplied by the value of money and that the actual wage was above or below the value of labor-power. In such a case there would be unequal exchange in the buying and selling of labor-power. Marx does not rule out the possibility of unequal exchange in the market for labor-power, but he is careful to explain the appropriation of surplus value on the basis of the assumption that labor-power, like other commodities, exchanges at its value.

The wage bargain provides a particular capitalist's workers with only the money wage agreed on, not with any claim to a part of that capitalist's product. Workers as a class, on the other hand, spend their wages to buy some part of the total product. Thus the value added in capitalist production must be thought of as being split between a fraction that workers receive in the form of wages and the surplus value that passes into the hands of the capitalists. The value of labor-power expresses this division of value added by measuring the fraction of value added that workers receive. We can also express this division of value added by the ratio of surplus value to wages, which Marx calls the *rate of surplus value, e*:

$$e = \text{surplus value} / \text{wages} \tag{3.5a}$$
$$= (1 - w^*)/w^* = (1 - mw)/mw$$
$$w^* = 1/(1 + e) \tag{3.5b}$$

This division of value added between wages and surplus value is characteristic of capitalist production. All commodity production exhibits the category of value added, which reflects the fact that in commodity production social labor takes the form of value. But it is only in capitalist production that the value added splits into these two fundamental parts, reflecting the fact that labor-power has become a commodity that is bought and sold on the market.

Surplus Value and Unpaid Labor   (Capital 1.10)

Marx proposes a powerful metaphor to help us understand the social significance of the emergence of labor-power as a commodity and the fact that the value of labor-power is "normally" less than 1, that is, that the rate of surplus value is normally greater than 0. He asks us to imagine the whole social labor time as one great "working day," which represents the social labor of the society, although we can also think of it as the day of the average laborer. This working day consists of a certain number of hours of social labor actually expended in production. Because labor time corresponds to value added in the aggregate in Marx's theory, the working day can also be thought of as the aggregate value added.

Because the value of labor-power equals less than 1 hour of social labor time equivalent received by workers per hour of social labor actually expended, we can think of the value of labor-power as dividing the working day, or the aggregate value added, into two parts (Figure 3.1). If we think of this division in terms of the value added, it is a division between wages on the one hand and surplus value on the other. If we think of it as a division of the working day, the first part of the working day is labor expended by workers for which they receive an equivalent in the wage. The second part of the working day (corresponding to surplus value) is labor expended by workers for which they receive no equivalent in the form of wages. Marx refers to these two parts as *paid labor time* and *unpaid labor time*, respectively. Thus the surplus value is the result of unpaid labor time.

Marx does not mean, of course, that in an hourly wage system workers are forced to work some hours for zero wages. Every hour of *labor-power* is paid for in the sense that the worker receives the hourly value of labor-power. But not every hour of *labor* is paid for

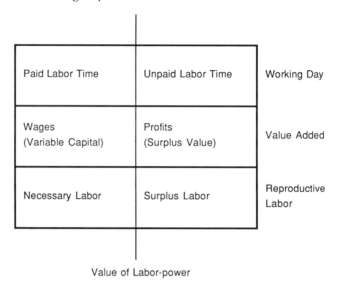

Figure 3.1.   Capitalist labor time

because the value of labor-power is less than one. Suppose that the value of money is 1/15 hour per dollar and that the average wage is $7.50 per hour. Then the value of labor-power is 1/2 hour of social labor per hour of labor-power sold. An average worker in an 8-hour day would produce $120 (8 hours × $15 per hour) of value added and receives $60 (8 hours × $7.50 per hour) in wages. Workers earning the average wage receive the equivalent of 4 hours of social labor per day in the form of the wage and work for 4 hours without receiving an equivalent compensation, even though every hour of labor-power is duly paid for at the average wage rate.

Marx implicitly assumes that the whole of social reproduction is mediated through the exchange of commodities, including the reproduction of labor-power, that is, the reproduction of people themselves. We can view the labor that produces what productive workers consume as the labor *necessary* for the reproduction of society and the labor that capitalists appropriate in the form of surplus value as the *surplus labor time* of the society, in the sense that only the necessary labor time would be required to enable reproduction of people and productive facilities on the same scale. Thus the wage-labor mechanism allows capitalists as a class to appropriate the surplus labor time of the society without giving workers as a class any equivalent.

A situation in which one person gives another something for which the giver receives no equivalent is commonly called *exploitation*. Because this is exactly the situation in capitalist production, Marx argues that, from the point of view of the labor theory of value, the source of surplus value lies in the exploitation of the laborer.

If you do not accept the postulate that labor produces the whole value added, you will not see much basis for the claim that wage-labor is exploitative. I think this is the main reason that the labor theory of value has fallen into disrepute among orthodox economists. To avoid the characterization of capitalist social relations as exploitative requires the construction of some other theory of value that makes the wage seem to be a complete social equivalent for the labor that workers actually perform.

Surplus, Exploitation, Class, and Surplus Value

There is considerable confusion about the relation between the concepts of social surplus product (or surplus), surplus value, and capitalist exploitation, so it is worth a moment's thought to clarify this issue.

Every human society that is capable of development and change produces a surplus product. If the productive powers of a society only allow it to produce what is necessary for its reproduction at the same level of development, there is no room for change or advance.

In many human societies, especially those that have left written historical records, the social surplus product is appropriated by one class of people through some specific mechanism. For example, in societies based on slavery, the entire labor of the slave is at the disposal of the master; hence the slave's surplus labor and the product it produces become the direct property of the master. In feudal society the surplus labor time of the serfs was appropriated by the lords through the requirement that serfs work a certain number of days a year on the lord's fields. The lord then directly appropriated the surplus labor through owning the product of those fields. Societies that are based on the appropriation of surplus product by a particular group of people Marx calls *class soci-*

eties. It is clear that class societies are based on one or another form of exploitation of workers.

Marx analyzes capitalist society as a class society. The specific mechanism by which the capitalists appropriate the surplus labor of the workers is the wage-labor system. Because the distinction between labor time and labor-power is subtle, the wage-labor form tends to obscure the fact that its result is exploitation. The capitalists as a class wind up with control over the surplus labor time of the society because they own the surplus value.

Two quite different senses can be attached to the idea of ending exploitation in capitalist society. If we were to try to end exploitation by raising the value of labor-power so that workers received in their wages the whole value added, we would destroy the capacity of the system to produce a social surplus product, because surplus value is the form the surplus product takes in a capitalist society. If, on the other hand, we wanted to maintain or strengthen the ability of the society to produce a surplus product, and at the same time end exploitation, we would have to alter the fundamental organization of production in such a way that the surplus no longer took the form of a surplus value appropriated by a particular class. This distinction was extremely important for Marx, who spent a lot of his political life fighting against socialists who wanted to solve the problem of exploitation without altering the wage-labor form of production.

A viable and developing socialist society would have to produce a surplus product, both to provide for social needs and to provide for expansion of productive resources. As a result, workers in a viable socialist society could not receive directly a claim to the whole product. Whether or not this constitutes exploitation of the workers in a socialist society depends on one's analysis of the mechanisms of control of the social surplus. Is it appropriated privately by a particular class or controlled, more or less effectively, by the workers as a whole? The mere fact that workers fail to receive the whole product directly does not constitute evidence of exploitation.

The Reproduction of Capital and the Reproduction of Society

As I mentioned earlier, in *Capital* Marx seems to assume that commodity relations are the only processes involved in the reproduction of capitalist society. This point is particularly clear in his willingness to identify the paid part of the capitalist working day with the labor time necessary for social reproduction. The difference between social reproduction as a whole and the part of social reproduction directly mediated by capitalist relations of production has become the focus of important political movements in the twentieth century. An important part of social reproduction is carried on outside capitalist relations of production. In advanced capitalist societies the most important part of this extra-capitalist labor is in household production and domestic labor, whereas in less developed capitalist societies an important part is in traditional peasant production. Furthermore, an important part of the consumption of workers in advanced capitalist societies has come to be mediated by the State; hence social consumption (public education, welfare and retirement benefits, public health, state-financed medical care, and so on) plays an important role in the reproduction of workers.

We need to modify Marx's diagram of the working day to reflect these developments. In Figure 3.2 the whole social working day is now divided into a wage-labor part and a non-wage-labor part. The value of labor-power in the narrow sense now divides only the wage-labor part of the working day into paid and unpaid fractions (remember that non-wage-labor is not the same as un-

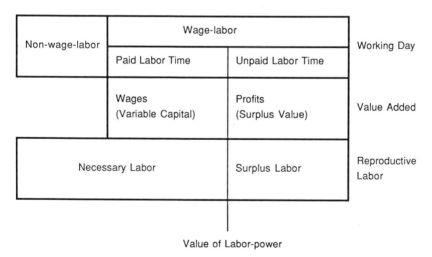

Value of Labor-power

Figure 3.2.   Social labor time

paid wage-labor). The necessary labor time of the society now includes necessary non-wage-labor and thus is larger than just the paid part of the wage-labor time. Some part of the paid wage-labor is consumed socially by workers, through paying taxes to the State and consuming State-provided goods. This portion is part of the paid, waged working day.

The Value of Labor-Power Again   *(Capital 1.6)*

One other point in Marx's treatment of the value of labor-power has produced considerable misunderstanding. We have expressed the value of labor-power as the amount of social labor time workers receive, in the form of the wage, in exchange for their labor-power. Marx, making (as he often does) the assumption that commodities exchange at prices that reflect the labor time expended on each commodity individually (equal exchange), emphasizes the idea that this labor time is directly embodied in the commodity labor-power:

> The value of labour-power is determined, as in the case of every other commodity, by the labour-time necessary for the production, and consequently also the reproduction, of this special article. So far as it has value, it represents no more than a definite quantity of the average labour of society incorporated in it. Labour-power exists only as a capacity, or power of the living individual . . . Given the individual, the production of labour-power consists in his reproduction of himself or his maintenance. For his maintenance he requires a given quantity of the means of subsistence. Therefore the labour-time requisite for the production of labour-power reduces itself to that necessary for the production of those means of subsistence; in other words, the value of labour-power is the value of the means of subsistence necessary for the maintenance of the labourer.   (1867, pp. 170–171)

Under the assumption of equal exchange, there are no problems with this formulation. Workers receive a certain amount of money in their wages, which is the equivalent (through the value of money) of a certain amount of labor time. Whatever commodities they spend their wages on contain an amount of labor exactly proportionate to their prices, because of the assumption of equal exchange; hence the workers actually consume in commodities the same amount of labor as that represented by their wages.

If we have a situation of unequal exchange, however, it is no longer certain that the commodities workers purchase with their wages will have prices that accurately represent the amount of labor they contain. Workers may wind up consuming somewhat more or somewhat less labor time in commodities than the equivalent of the wage, because they, like all other agents in a commodity economy, may gain or lose from unequal exchange.

Thus it is important to think of the value of labor-power first as the amount of average social labor workers receive a claim to in the wage for each hour they actually work—that is, as the average wage multiplied by the value of money—rather than as the labor contained in the commodities workers consume.

In a long-run perspective it is reasonable to suppose that the main determinant of the value of labor-power is the cost of maintaining the average social standard of living of the workers, as Marx goes on to suggest:

> the number and extent of [the worker's] so-called necessary wants, as also the modes of satisfying them, are themselves the product of historical development, and depend therefore to a great extent on the degree of civilisation of a country, more particularly on the conditions under which, and consequently on the habits and degree of comfort in which, the class of free labourers has been formed. In contradistinction therefore to the case of other commodities, there enters into the determination of the value of labour-power a historical and moral element. Nevertheless, in a given country, at a given period, the average quantity of means of subsistence necessary for the labourer is practically known.   (1867, p. 171)

And, we might add, the cost of those means of subsistence, given the patterns of unequal exchange prevalent in that country, is also known.

It is important to be cautious with Marx's formulation that labor-power is like any other commodity. From the point of view of the capitalist, this is largely true, because the capitalist's only interest in labor-power is its money cost and the value it can produce. But even for the capitalist there are important differences between labor-power and other commodities, especially the fact that even after the wage bargain has been struck, there continues to be a conflict between worker and capitalist over the intensity and conditions of labor. From a social point of view, labor-power is emphatically not like other commodities. It is produced in very different relations of production—normally, for example, without the appropriation of surplus value by anybody in the process of its production. The production of labor-power viewed socially is the reproduction of people and their talents, capacities, and consciousness, a much more complex and awesome phenomenon even than the production of commodities.

Expanding (Variable) and Nonexpanding (Constant) Capital   (Capital 1.8)

The capitalist advances capital both to buy labor-power and to buy nonlabor means of production, including investment in long-lived equipment and buildings. From the capitalist's point of view, both outlays are equally necessary for profitable production.

The labor theory of value, on the other hand, suggests that these two types of advance are different from a social point of view. The value of nonlabor means of production appears unchanged in the price of the finished commodity. The value advanced to purchase labor-power, on the other hand, reappears in the price of the finished commodity expanded by the amount of surplus value the unpaid labor of the workers has added to it. Marx calls the capital advanced for nonlabor means of production *constant capital*, because it does not expand in the process of production; and he calls the capital advanced to purchase labor-power *variable capital*, because this value does expand through production.

For example, suppose that in a certain year an average capitalist firm spent $100 million on nonlabor inputs to production, of which $20 million was depreciation on long-lived plant and equipment, $80 million was spent on raw materials used up in the production process, and $50 million was spent on the wages of production workers. If the firm sold its finished commodities for $200 million, we would view $100 million of that total price as a recovery of the costs of nonlabor inputs, or constant capital, $50 million as the equivalent of the wages paid, or variable capital, and $50 million as surplus value. The value added would be $200 million less $100 million purchased inputs, or $100 million. Thus Marx expresses the total price of commodities as:

$$c + v + s \tag{3.6}$$

where c is constant capital (in this case, $100 million), v is variable capital (in this case, $50 million) and s is surplus value (in this case, also $50 million). The value added is $v + s$, or $100 million in the example.

The capitalist expresses the surplus value as a percentage of the total capital advanced and calls this percentage the *markup on costs*. The markup on costs is

$$q = s/(c+v) \tag{3.7}$$

which in this example is $1/3 = $50 million/$150 million.

From the point of view of the labor theory of value, the capacity of the capitalist system to produce surplus value depends on the rate of surplus value, $e = s/v$ (because that measures the amount by which variable capital expands in the production process), and on the *composition of capital*, $k = v/(c + v)$ (because that number expresses the proportion of the total capital outlays that actually go to purchase labor-power and hence the proportion of each dollar of capital that actually expands in the production process). (Marx often refers to the ratio $c/v = (1-k)/k$ as the *organic composition of capital*. A *fall* in k, the composition of capital, corresponds to a *rise* in c/v.) There is an identity relating the markup to the rate of surplus value and the composition of capital:

$$q = s/(c+v) = (s/v)[v/(c + v)] = ek \tag{3.8}$$

It is important not to confuse constant capital and variable capital with *fixed capital* (capital tied up in long-lived plant and equipment) and *circulating capital* (capital that turns over rapidly in production, such as wages and the value of raw materials). The depreciation on fixed capital is part of constant capital, but by no means all of it, because capital advanced to buy raw materials and other rapidly used inputs to production are also part of constant capital. The wages of production workers are a part of circulating capital, but not the whole, because circulating capital also includes the value of raw materials.

To get some sense of the magnitudes of these variables in contemporary capitalist production, we can look at the U.S. Census Bureau's *Annual Survey of Manufactures*. This survey asks every U.S. manufacturing establishment to report the value of its total output, its production wages, its nonproduction wages, its spending on purchased inputs to production, and its new investment in plant and equipment each year. From these figures it is possible to calculate the division of the price of manufactured products among the c, v, and s categories. For 1974, for example, we have, in billions of dollars,

Value of finished commodities	$c+v+s$	$1034.2
Wages of production workers	v	125.0
Purchases of inputs	c_1	581.7
Depreciation (estimated)	c_2	13.4
Constant capital ($c_1 + c_2$)	c	595.1
Surplus value	s	314.1
Value added	$s+v$	439.1

where c_1 is the part of constant capital that goes to rapidly used-up inputs and c_2 is the part that represents the depreciation of long-lived plant and equipment.

The rate of surplus value (s/v) in U.S. manufacturing in 1974 was 2.51 (251%); the value of labor-power ($v/(s + v)$) in the narrow sense was 0.28; the composition of capital ($v/(c + v)$) was 0.17 (17% of capital outlays went to production labor); and the markup ($s/(c + v)$) was 0.44 (44%) $= 2.51 \times 0.17$. Production workers worked about 11.2 hours of a standard 40-hour week for themselves and about 28.8 hours to produce surplus value. But only about 1/6 of the total capital advanced went to purchase labor-power; hence the overall rate of expansion of capital was 44%: each $1 advanced resulted in $1.44 returning to the capitalist firms in sales.

Historical changes in the rate of surplus value and in the composition of costs play a major role in the evolution of the total profitability of the system of capital and reflect basic changes in the standard of living of workers, the productivity of labor, and the technology of production.

The Explanation of Surplus Value

Marx's explanation of the origin of surplus value within the framework of the labor theory of value is of central importance to his analysis of capitalist production. Essentially, the rest of his work consists of an attempt to apply this theory to explain the actual phenomena of capitalist production.

The basic points in this explanation are, first, the idea that in the aggregate, commodities exchange at their values so that value is conserved in exchange; and, second, the distinction between labor-power (the commodity that is available to capitalists on the market) and labor (the actual expenditure of human effort in production that adds value to commodities). Surplus value is possible in the system as long as the value of labor-power is less than 1. Under these circumstances, which emerge historically through the creation of a mass of workers free to sell their labor-power and with no access to their own means of production, the surplus value appropriated by the capitalists is the result of exploitation. Workers work more hours than they receive an equivalent for in the form of the wage.

Thus the capitalist system of production, although appearing on the surface to establish an equality between all individuals as property owners (even if their property consists only of their own labor-power), rests on the private appropriation of the social surplus product by a particular class. The form through which this exploitation takes place, the selling of labor-power for a wage and the appropriation of surplus value, is specifically characteristic of capitalist production. Capitalist society develops and reproduces itself through this fundamentally contradictory process.

Neoclassical Theories of Surplus Value

It is interesting to note that neoclassical economic theory tries to explain surplus value in capitalist production within a framework of exchange of equivalents. In neoclassical economic theory, surplus value (or the profit of capital) is merely a special case of the exchange of goods and services between different time periods. The capitalist is merely, in this theory, buying labor today and selling output tomorrow. Because people prefer to consume earlier rather than later, the price of a commodity today is higher than the price of the same commodity tomorrow. Thus, if one unit of labor exchanges for one unit of output today and one unit of output today exchanges for two units of output tomorrow because of time preference, the capitalist who buys one unit of labor, uses it in production, and as a result has two units of output (worth two units of labor) tomorrow will be no better off than the worker who simply consumes a unit of output today. Because the two units of output (which include the Marxian surplus value) exist in a different time period, they are viewed as the equivalent of one unit of output in the present.

It is not clear that these two analyses are contradictory, although they give different interpretations of the same situation. The question is why there should be a discount of future goods and services against present ones. Neoclassical economic theory attributes this to the psychology of the agents, especially of the capitalists, in a context of full employment of all resources. Marxist theory argues that, on the contrary, there is no tendency for capitalist systems to employ all available resources and that the psychology of capitalists is determined by the possibility of appropriating surplus value, not the other way around. The root of this disagreement lies in the different theories of value adopted by the two schools and in the consequent different interpretations of equivalence among commodities. Neoclassical theory sees goods and services as equivalents from the subjective point of view of the consumer; Marx sees them as equivalents in the objective sense that they carry a certain part of the social labor time of the society. The same phenomenon (appropriation of surplus value) can be seen as the exchange of subjective equivalents and as objective exploitation.

4

Production under Capitalism

Absolute and Relative Surplus Value   *(Capital 1.12)*

Marx identifies the fulcrum of capitalist society as the appropriation of surplus value and the source of surplus value in the exploitation of workers through the institution of wage-labor. We now turn our attention to Marx's analysis of the influence of these structural features of capitalist production on the development of productive techniques and organization.

In Marx's analysis the social surplus value depends on two factors: the total social labor time, and the partitioning of that labor time between paid and unpaid labor, a division determined by the value of labor-power. The value of labor-power, in turn, depends on the relation between the average standard of living of workers in a particular society at a particular time and the ability of labor to produce use-values, because these factors determine the portion of the social labor time that has to be devoted to producing the use-values workers need to maintain their standard of living. As Figures 4.1 and 4.2 indicate, the social surplus value can be expanded either by increasing the total social labor time while holding the part devoted to paid labor constant, or by reducing the part of the social labor time that is paid while holding the total labor time constant, or by a combination of these two methods.

Lengthening the social labor time without increasing the paid labor portion is possible because, given the means of subsistence necessary to maintain their basic standard of living, workers are

physically able to provide more or less labor time to social production. Thus there is room for a struggle between workers and
capitalists over how much labor time will be extracted in exchange
for the wage. The increase in total social labor time, holding the
paid portion constant, Marx calls *absolute surplus value.*

Shortening the paid portion of the social labor time is possible,
given the standard of living of workers, only if the labor time
required to produce the commodities workers consume to maintain their standard of living declines. This decline takes place constantly in capitalist production through technical changes that
increase the productivity of labor. Marx calls the shortening of the
paid part of the social labor time through increased labor productivity *relative surplus value.*

Forms of Absolute Surplus Value   (Capital 1.10)

The simplest form of absolute surplus value is when workers are
required to work long hours in each day, week, or year. Within
broad limits, the extension of the working day to 10, 12, or 14
hours and of the working week to 60, 72, or 100 hours does not
greatly decrease the effectiveness of the workers, especially in
routine jobs, and does not greatly increase the quantity of means
of subsistence they require. In fact, by reducing free time, the

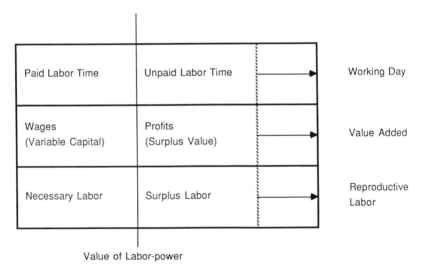

Figure 4.1.   Absolute surplus value

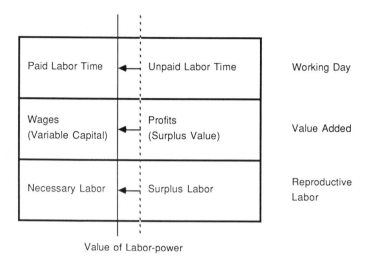

Figure 4.2.   Relative surplus value

extension of the working day may reduce workers' consumption needs to some degree. This extension is a pervasive tendency of capitalist production in its early phases.

The length of the working day has absolute limits, of course. Eventually workers become so exhausted and inattentive that their productivity falls and may become negative, for example, when the value of the machinery and raw materials they destroy is greater than the value of the usable product. Before this absolute limit is reached, however, the only limit to the length of the working day will be the workers' resistance to capitalists' demands.

The power of workers to resist long hours depends on their general bargaining power in relation to employers and especially on their solidarity. An individual worker is in a very weak bargaining position with regard to hours in industrial production. The capitalist plans production around a certain shift length. He offers the worker a take-it-or-leave-it proposition: to work the standard shift or not to work at all. The costs to the capitalist of making exceptions to the standard working day for individual workers are high, because when one or a few workers leave early they must be replaced for awkward fragments of the working day if their departure is not to disrupt the whole production process. The power of workers as a group to bargain over the working day is much greater. The capitalist obviously prefers a longer to a shorter shift but prefers a somewhat shorter shift to no production at all.

The struggle over the length of the working day was a key element in the formation of labor unions in industrial capitalist countries. In most advanced countries these struggles reached such a pitch of conflict that the State stepped in to regulate the length of the working day by establishing a norm and requiring employers to pay a fine to workers (such as the time-and-a-half for overtime familiar in the United States) for exceeding the norm.

Lengthened work time is the most obvious form of absolute surplus value. It has seen a revival in less advanced capitalist countries with newly formed industrial labor forces, massive unemployment, and procapitalist, antiunion, authoritarian governments, where workers' ability to resist long hours is very weak.

Another form of absolute surplus value involves the elimination of unproductive periods in the working day: coffee breaks, informal socializing of workers, rest periods, and the like. Clearly the principles involved in bargaining between workers and capitalists over these periods are exactly the same as the principles involved in bargaining over the total length of the working day: the capitalist wants to maximize the unpaid labor time by extracting as much labor as possible from workers without increasing the wage.

It may be less obvious that the length of the working day is also the central issue behind struggles over children's and women's labor. The wage is the source of means of subsistence for the workers' families rather than just means of subsistence for the individual worker. What the capitalist cares about is how much social labor time the whole family performs in exchange for the family wage. If all members of the family work for wages, the total wage paid to enable them to subsist will not increase as much as the total labor time they supply. Instead of paying one worker the $15,000 necessary to support a family at modest standards of living in exchange for 2,000 hours of labor-power a year, the capitalist may be able to pay one family worker $12,000 and another $8,000 in exchange for 4,000 hours of labor-power. The effect from the point of view of the capitalist is to expand absolute surplus value because the total social labor time increases without a proportionate increase in paid labor time.

This link between family labor and the conditions of exploitation has had an important impact on political struggles over the status of women and women's role in the labor market. Nineteenth- and early twentieth-century efforts on the part of labor to limit and regulate the exploitation of workers recognized the link between family labor and the social working day. Campaigns to limit or abolish the exploitation of women and children were often connected to campaigns to limit the working day. The resolution of these problems eventually reached by largely male unions in their negotiations with male capitalists was to limit the exploitation of families by putting restrictions on the use of women's and children's labor-power. In this way the family was offered some protection from the pressures to expand the family working day, but at the expense of the rights of women to enter the labor market on the same terms as men.

This drama continues in the last part of the twentieth century with the gradual dismantling of "protective" legislation that restricts the ability of women and children to enter the labor market on the same terms as adult men. On the one hand this has eliminated an important source of sexual inequality; on the other, it has led to a renewal of the basic pressures for absolute surplus value through the expansion of the total labor time families supply to the labor market. An important aspect in this development has been the emergence of the two-income family as a social norm.

Relative Surplus Value   *(Capital 1.12)*

The second pervasive tendency within capitalist production is to increase the rate of surplus value. Capitalist production is inherently dynamic or, as Marx and Engels put it in the *Communist Manifesto* (1848), revolutionary. Old methods of production are constantly being scrapped in favor of new ones, which often involve a larger scale of production. The net result is either a shortening of the labor time necessary to produce a given set of use-values or the substitution of entirely new products for existing ones, both changes enabling people to satisfy their needs in new ways that cost less labor to produce.

This process has an effect on value production only insofar as it changes the proportions in which the social working day is divided between surplus value and wages, or between paid and unpaid labor time. If the value of labor-power is regulated by the labor time it takes to produce the commodities necessary for workers to maintain their average standard of living, then a reduction in the labor time necessary to produce these commodities will also lower the value of labor-power and increase the rate of surplus value.

It is important to see that it is possible, with increases in labor productivity, for the real wages or standard of living of workers to rise at the same time that the value of labor-power declines. Some part of the increased productivity of labor may go to raising the real consumption of workers, but the means of subsistence still may become so much cheaper that the value of labor-power declines. Different historical phases of capital accumulation have been characterized by different patterns in this respect. For example, it was the conscious idea of many U.S. capitalists in the first decades of the twentieth century to sponsor a rise in workers' standards of living, partly to create a mass market for consumer durable products like automobiles and partly because they calculated that such a rise would be accompanied by an even greater rise in the productivity of labor, and hence by an increase in surplus value. Some modern Marxist analysts call this phenomenon "Fordism" (Aglietta, 1979).

Technical Progress: Use-Value and Value   (Capital 1.12)

It is worth considering at this point exactly what effects technical progress has in value theory terms. We shall also return to this problem when we study Marx's discussion of the tendency of the rate of profit to fall in the course of capital accumulation.

Technical change under capitalism is motivated by individual capitalists' attempts to lower their costs of production. Any particular capitalist who succeeds in discovering a method of lowering costs of production benefits for a longer or shorter time by appropriating a "super-profit," because his commodities continue to sell for the same market price as those of other capitalists' but his costs of production are smaller. In value theory terms this super-profit is a part of the social surplus value that the innovating capitalist appropriates through unequal exchange. This super-profit inevitably declines over time as other capitalists discover the same or even more effective techniques for lowering costs. In the end the price of the commodity produced is forced down by competition to reflect the new, lower costs of its production.

Not all cost-reducing innovations are based on the saving of labor in production. Some changes of technique reduce the wear-

and-tear on machinery and tools or the wastage of raw material in a production process and hence reduce costs in those ways. But many cost-reducing innovations do result in a lower necessary labor time to produce given use-values. Thus the consequence of these innovations is a decline not only in the price but also in the labor value of the commodities. Marx focuses particular attention on such labor-economizing innovations.

There is a difference between the use-value productivity of labor and the amount of value labor produces. From the point of view of the labor theory of value, an hour of social labor time always produces the same amount of value although the monetary representation of that value may change if the value of money changes. Thus technical progress cannot increase the amount of value an hour of social labor produces. It can, of course, greatly increase the amount of any specific use-value, say, cars or food, that can be produced with an hour of social labor. A fundamental insight of the labor theory of value is that technical progress has the primary effect of lowering the value of commodities by reducing the amount of social labor required to produce them.

This point is reflected in the fact that the primary effect of technical change is to lower the prices of commodities. Suppose that in a certain society the price of wheat accurately reflects the labor embodied in it; thus the price of wheat is equal to its value divided by the value of money. Suppose that the value of money is 1/15 hour of social labor per dollar. Suppose further that initially it takes an hour of direct labor to produce 10 bushels of wheat and that the other inputs required cost $15, thus representing another hour of indirect labor contained in the wheat. The price of the wheat under equal exchange will be $30, comprising $15 to recover the costs of nonlabor inputs and $15 of value added. If the value of labor-power is 1/2, the wage will be $7.50 an hour, and the $15 of value added will be divided into $7.50 of wages and $7.50 of surplus value. The cost of 10 bushels of wheat to the capitalist producer is $22.50.

Suppose now that a new technique is discovered that permits the same 10 bushels of wheat to be produced with 2/3 hour of direct labor. Initially the cost of producing 10 bushels of wheat will decline to $20 ($15 of nonlabor inputs and $5 of wages), and the surplus value will rise to $10. But competition between the capitalists will tend to drive the price down. The labor theory of value argues that the price must eventually fall to the point where the value added in the 10 bushels of wheat equals the direct labor time multiplied by the value of money. Thus the price would eventually settle at $25, equal to the $15 of costs of nonlabor inputs plus $10 representing 2/3 hour of social labor time directly applied in producing the wheat. This $10 of value added will be divided into $5 of wages and $5 of surplus value. It is instructive to notice in this example that the markup on costs has declined. Originally the markup on costs $(s/(c+v))$ was $7.50/$22.50 = 1/3 and in the new situation will be $5/$20 = 1/4. This change is due to the fact that even though the rate of surplus value has remained the same, 1, the composition of capital has fallen from 1/3 ($7.50/$22.50) to 1/4 ($5/$20).

After the technical change a given amount of social labor produces the same amount of value as before, despite the fact that that same hour produces 50% more use-values (bushels of wheat). If we want to find some effect of technical progress of this kind on capitalist production in value terms, then we must look at the secondary effects of these changes on the value of labor-power, because the value of labor-power will determine the division of value added between wages and surplus value. If, for example, bread made from wheat is a very important part of workers' standard of living, we would expect the cheapening of wheat to be reflected in a lower cost of bread and in lower wages. The cost of wheat has fallen by $5 for 10 bushels, or 16% (1/6) from its original price of $30. If wheat were the only commodity that workers consumed and the standard of living of workers remained constant, we would expect the wage to fall by 1/6 as well, from $7.50 an hour of labor-power to $6.25 an hour. Then the value of labor-power would fall from 1/2 to 5/12 (0.42). The surplus value in 10 bushels of wheat would rise from $5 to $5.83 ($4.17 of wages), and the markup on costs would rise to 29%, still lower than the original 1/3, because the composition of capital has fallen to 1/4.

This example shows some of the central presumptions Marx has about technical progress in capitalism. The main effect of technical innovations is to reduce the labor time required to produce use-values, but capitalists cannot directly benefit from this change because competition will force prices in the aggregate to reflect values. The indirect effect of technical progress is to cheapen the means of subsistence that workers consume. This change would allow either a rise in workers' standards of living, or a fall in the value of labor-power, or some combination of the two. The net effect of these latter changes is a rise in the rate of surplus value as a result of a fall in the value of labor-power. But a fall in the composition of capital leads to a lower markup after all the adjustments have been achieved.

The Capitalist and the Form of Production (Capital 1.13)

The development of modern industrial production took place under capitalist social relations of production. Many people are tempted to think that the productivity of modern industry is inextricably linked to capitalist social relations of production and that human beings cannot achieve high levels of social productivity in any other form of productive organization. Furthermore, capitalists perform several critical roles in the initiation and organization of production: they are the entrepreneurs who set in motion the enormous productive forces of capitalist society. It appears at first sight that to do away with capitalists as a class would be to do away with large-scale production altogether and with their innovations and organization.

Marx is at pains to rebut these presumptions. He wants to show that the link between capitalist social relations and the development of productive forces is a historic, not a structural, connection. He argues that a socialist society could organize production better—more productively and more rationally—than capitalist society can. To make this argument he must convince us that large-scale productive enterprise is possible without capitalists. Marx tries to establish this idea through a historical examination of the role capitalists have played in shaping and organizing production. He sums up his general point of view on the relation of the capitalist to production in *Capital* (1867, p. 332): "It is not because he is a leader of industry that a man is a capitalist; on the contrary, he is a leader of industry because he is a capitalist. The leadership of industry is an attribute of capital, just as in feudal times the functions of general and judge were attributes of landed property."

Marx's view of the interplay between capitalist social relations and the development of productive forces under capitalist leadership is extremely subtle and complex. The capitalist develops productive forces; but because his direct motive is the pursuit of surplus value, the development of production is a by-product. Furthermore, the fact that surplus value is the capitalist's aim puts him (or his agents) in direct conflict with the actual producers—workers—over wages, length of the working day, intensity of work, and the safety and healthiness of the working environment. It is out of this interplay of contradictory forces that the shape of modern industrial production emerges.

Although we might suppose at first that increases in the productivity of labor would always be to the capitalist's advantage, a closer look at the situation reveals some counteracting factors. The capitalist has to retain control over the pace and intensity of work. But some innovations may raise productivity by increasing workers' autonomy over the production process; hence they may not increase surplus value because they sacrifice too much control over the labor process. The most successful innovations in capitalist production, for example, the assembly line, combine substantial increases in labor productivity with built-in elements of surveillance and control over the pace and intensity of labor. The failure of an individual worker on an assembly line to match the pace set by the line is immediately apparent and policeable. Hence we have a development of productive forces, but one that is shaped distinctively by the social relations of capitalism.

The development of productive forces under capitalism represents an enormous development of human power to control and shape the physical environment. But this social development does not correspond directly to the individual human development of the workers. The capitalist, because he has his eye on surplus value, cannot afford to pay attention to the effects of the labor process on the workers as human beings. Thus decisions that drastically diminish workers' human lives are routinely taken in the hope of increasing surplus value. Marx does not deny the need for powerful social techniques of innovation and organization in modern industry. He does question whether these functions can be left in the hands of capitalists who are motivated by the pursuit of surplus value and whose ideology celebrates the separation of their decisions from any consideration of the direct human consequences of their actions. Would not workers be better served by managers who were answerable to them in terms of the specific decisions about the organization of production? Might not society come to a point where the private organization of production came into unavoidable conflicts with the social effects of production?

The Pattern of Capitalist Development
of Production   *(Capital 1.13, 1.14, 1.15)*

Marx analyzes the problems of capitalist organization of production in three masterful chapters on *cooperation, manufacture,* and *machine production.*

In cooperation the worker and her productive process are brought together with other, similar workers, but without any fundamental change in the method of production. The advantage for the capitalist of gathering workers together is the increased control and surveillance over the work process, the release of human energy from the social interaction of the workers, and the saving in shared facilities—buildings, heat, and so forth—available in this way. In addition, some simple forms of joint labor become possible because of the gathering together of workers. Marx gives the example of stone masons who form a line to hand stones up to the working point on the top of a wall and in this way greatly shorten the time and effort needed to move the stones. The important point is that cooperation requires very little specialization of workers. The labor is shared, but the workers are functionally interchangeable.

Manufacture, on the other hand, involves a reorganization of the method of production and the extreme specialization of workers to particular aspects of the productive process. This is *division of labor* in the classic Smithian sense. Not only the workers' skills but also their tools become highly specialized. Marx makes an important distinction between the principles underlying division of labor in manufacture and those underlying division of labor in society. The division of labor in society is regulated by the market, through the exchange of commodities, whereas the division of labor in production is regulated by the direct authority of the capitalist as the initiator and director of the production process. The increases in production possible with manufacture are great, but the costs in the human development of the workers are great as well: "In manufacture, in order to make the collective labourer, and through him capital, rich in social productive power, each labourer must be made poor in individual productive powers" (Marx, 1867, p. 361).

The specialization of workers in manufacture leads eventually to problems for the capitalist because specialized workers can organize effectively to monopolize certain skills and functions. Manufacture as a form of organization of production is extremely vulnerable to such combinations of workers because the withdrawal of one productive function stops production altogether and because it is not easy to find alternative sources of the skills developed by the individual worker.

The advent of machine production brings both a massive increase in social productivity through increases in the scale of production and in the mechanical power at labor's disposal and a partial solution to the capitalist's problems with worker organization under manufacture. The machine embodies the specialization of particular tasks characteristic of manufacture but generalizes the living worker's labor. The worker now becomes a machine tender, and, as such, relatively moveable from one type of machine to another. The special function in production has moved from the worker's brain and hand to the machine itself. Thus at the same time that capitalism reaches its peak of productivity in the use of machines, it produces the desperate human problems of the modern proletariat. The worker has no organic relation to the process of production and no special bargaining position to shield her from the vicissitudes of the market. It is easy to train new machine operatives if the existing ones refuse to work and to shift workers from one work station to another as the need arises. This decline in the bargaining power of labor vis-a-vis capital leads directly to a lengthening of the work day and a deterioration in the conditions of work. We reach the characteristic modern situation of the human being who participates in fabulously powerful methods of production and is personally miserable in her work.

Conclusions

The problems we have discussed here are of central importance to Marx's vision of capitalism as a mode of production. They have less to do with formal issues like the theory of value and its relation to capitalist accounting practice than with the substantive question of the specific character of capitalist production.

For Marx capitalism differs from earlier class systems in that it puts each member of the dominant class under strong pressures to change the techniques and organization of production. This pressure is revolutionary and not always to the benefit of each capitalist, because the resulting revolutions in production always ruin some fortunes as they build up others. But these pressures give rise to the characteristic shaping of production under capitalist relations of production.

Marx categorizes the changes in social production broadly into two categories: those increasing absolute surplus value by extracting more labor from workers without changing the wage and those increasing relative surplus value through lowering the value of labor-power by reducing the cost of workers' consumption. The innovations that promote relative surplus value are connected with the fundamental tendency of capitalism to promote technical changes.

Furthermore, Marx argues that we can read the history of the evolution of production and work in terms of the specifically capitalist character of production. The movement from cooperative forms of production to manufacture marks the first intervention capitalism makes in the organization of production. Manufacture itself conflicts with the principles of capitalist production because it gives highly specialized craft workers too much power in the production process; this conflict is an important reason for the emergence of machine production.

The most important conclusion Marx draws from this study is that a socialist society would have substantial latitude in deciding the direction of technical change and the form of organization. It would not want to revive the older forms of production out of nostalgia for their human values, but it might try to incorporate some of the positive human and social characteristics of earlier modes of production into the development of a socialist mode of production that employed the most advanced possibilities of technology.

5

The Reproduction of Capital

The point of view of reproduction is central to Marx's theoretical thinking about human society: relations or forms exist in time in human society because they reproduce themselves in a systematic fashion. Marx felt that knowledge of these phenomena of human society is acquired through an understanding of this systematic process of reproduction. Indeed, the point of view of reproduction can transform our understanding of many phenomena. For example, the isolated sale of labor-power for a wage appears at first to be simply another instance of commodity exchange between formally equal owners of commodities. The capitalist begins the transaction with money and the worker with labor-power, and the two, like the exchangers of any other commodity, strike a bargain. But the repetition of this transaction gives it an entirely new and deeper significance. The capitalist at the end of the production cycle owns the commodities produced and can realize the full value of those commodities, including the surplus value in them. The average worker at the end of the production cycle has reproduced himself without having anything left over. Thus the capitalist is in a position to reproduce his activities on a larger scale, and the worker once again confronts the necessity of selling his labor-power in order to survive. When capitalist production is the chief method of organizing social production, the result is the appropriation by the capitalists as a class of the social surplus product in the form of surplus value. As this process repeats itself, it becomes clear that all the capitalists' value comes to be accumulated surplus value.

Thus for Marx the reproduction of capital is fundamentally the reproduction of the class relations of capitalist production. It is only in the repetition of the sale of labor-power that the class relations of capitalist society emerge, and the key to understanding capitalist production is to see how the production process itself reproduces workers and capitalists as separate classes: "The labourer therefore constantly produces material, objective wealth, but in the form of capital, of an alien power that dominates and exploits him; and the capitalist as constantly produces labour-power, but in the form of a subjective source of wealth, separated from the objects in and by which it can alone be realised; in short he produces the labourer, but as a wage-labourer" (Marx, 1867, p. 571).

Reproduction and Accumulation   *(Capital 1.24, 1.25)*

In capitalist production a proportion of the surplus value appropriated by capital is recommitted to the production process. We might call this process the *monetary aspect of capital accumulation*— the growth in the value of capital itself as a result of the reinvestment of surplus value. If the reinvested surplus value were merely to expand the capital's existing operations (building factories of exactly the same type and size, but more of them, for example), both constant and variable capital would grow in the same proportions. If wages were to remain constant, the total labor-power purchased (or in modern language, total employment) would grow at the same rate. This (imaginary) situation Marx calls *expanded reproduction*. It corresponds to the extension of capitalist social relations to more and more people, and to more and more aspects of people's lives, without any inner change in the structure of capital.

But real accumulation always involves a transformation of the processes of production. Capital is not satisfied simply to recreate on a larger scale what it has already achieved; rather it presses to adopt new methods of production and to exploit the possibilities of larger scale production. The extension of capitalist relations of production through accumulation creates a wider market that can support a deeper social division of labor, larger scale plants, machine production, and so on. The expansion of scale of production through the growth of individual capitals Marx calls *concentration* of capital. Accumulation also involves increases in productive scale through the agglomeration of existing capitals by means of (in modern financial terms) merger or acquisition. Marx calls this the *centralization* of capital. Thus accumulation is far from being a simple repetition of social production on a larger scale. Behind the monetary aspect of accumulation there is a fundamental change in the structure and organization of capital and equally fundamental changes in the scale and methods of production.

These changes in the production process are reflected in monetary terms in changes in the parameters that govern the profitability of capital, especially changes in the rate of surplus value and in the composition of capital, as our discussion of relative surplus value has already illustrated.

To separate levels of analysis, Marx distinguishes between reproduction and accumulation proper. In models of reproduction we abstract from the changes in the structure and organization of production that accompany real accumulation and assume that the parameters of the capitalist production process remain constant despite changes in scale. In the *simple reproduction model*, capitalists consume all the social surplus value; hence none is reinvested, and production continues at exactly the same scale, investment serving only to replace means of production used up in the last period. In the *expanded reproduction model*, reinvestment of some proportion of the surplus value occurs, but the parameters governing capital profitability, including the rate of surplus value and the composition of capital, remain invariant. *Accumulation models*, on the other hand, reflect the full impact of accumulation on all aspects of capitalist production and allow for changes in the underlying parameters. Clearly, we would not expect crises to appear in models of simple or expanded reproduction, but only in full models of accumulation.

Wages and the Reserve Army of Labor   (Capital 1.19, 1.25.3)

Accumulation has contrary effects on the demand for labor-power. On the one hand, the expansion of capital value through the reinvestment of surplus value tends to increase the demand for labor-power. The capitalist, in expanding production, normally needs to increase the amount of labor he uses. On the other hand, the changes in the technique of production that accompany accumulation usually involve the displacement of labor in production because technical improvements allow a smaller amount of labor to produce any given quantity of use-values. We can see the predominance of first one and then the other of these tendencies in the alternation between labor shortage and growing unemployment in developed capitalist economies.

The displacement of labor through technical change creates a pool of people who have been and usually need to be employed as wage-laborers but who cannot for the moment find a job. This pool of unemployed workers is a characteristic feature of capitalist production. Marx calls this pool the *floating reserve army of labor.* This pool is drawn down when accumulation creates more jobs than it destroys and is replenished when the opposite happens.

In addition to this floating reserve army Marx identifies two other major components of the relative surplus population in capitalist societies. Those people who reproduce themselves outside specifically capitalist relations of production, for example, in traditional agriculture, can be drawn or pushed into selling their labor-power. They thus form a *latent reserve army.* In twentieth-century capitalist economies this latent reserve army often exists in another, less developed country, and the drawing in of labor-power takes the form of migration. The supply of labor-power to the U.S. economy from Mexico and the Caribbean in the 1970s and 80s and the use of "guest workers" from Southern Europe and Northern Africa in Northern Europe in the 1960s are examples of this process. In countries in which women have low labor force participation rates, the potential supply of female labor-power can be an important part of the latent reserve army.

Finally, Marx discusses the *stagnant reserve army,* namely, those people whose labor-power deteriorates or whose skills are never developed or become obsolescent and who exist on the extreme margins of social production and organized social life.

The existence and constant renewal of the reserve army of labor is an important determinant of the level of wages; the reserve army explains why Marx views wages as tending to the cost of a socially determined subsistence standard of living. The potential and actual competition from the floating and latent reserve armies of labor prevents wages from rising very much or for very long above the historically determined average standard of living.

The Circuit of Capital   *(Capital 2.1–2.4, 2.7)*

We now turn from a general consideration of capital accumulation to the construction of some specific models of different aspects of the process. The easiest models to work with are, as Marx himself argues, models of reproduction in which the parameters of profitability remain constant in the face of the growth of capitalized value rather than models that try to reflect the full complexity of accumulation by allowing those parameters to change.

The basic conceptual tool Marx develops to approach the problem of accumulation is the *circuit of capital*. We have already seen that each individual capital can be thought of as value passing through the phases of the production process:

$$M - C\{MP,LP\} \ldots (P) \ldots C' - M' \tag{5.1}$$

Of course, a given capitalist firm may have several such cycles of production operating simultaneously, with the value in a different phase in each cycle. In fact, industrial capital normally has an essentially continuous flow of value passing through the production cycle, with new value constantly entering in the form of money and finished products constantly emerging from the production process.

We can think of the circuit of social capital as the combined circuits of all the individual capitals that make up the whole. Then it is natural to think of the capitalist production process as a closed circuit, with the different forms of capital—financial capital, productive capital, and commercial capital—at the three main nodes, as in Figure 5.1.

The *financial capital* node of the diagram corresponds to the M and M' that appear in expression (5.1). This capital is value in the form of money (money, that is, in the broad sense of any money-denominated financial asset), and the *capitalist* spends this money to buy labor-power and means of production (including gross investment in long-lived means of production). (Marx calls financial capital *money capital*.) The second node is *productive capital*, which consists of inventories of raw materials and partly finished goods and stocks of undepreciated plant and equipment. The finished

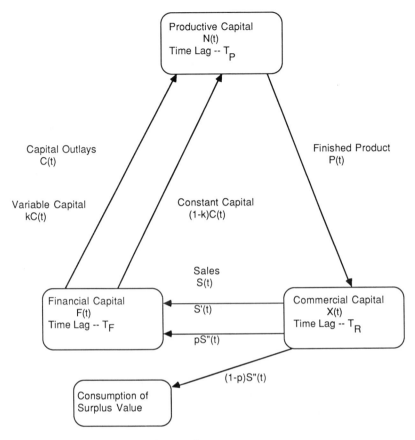

Figure 5.1.   The circuit of capital

product emerges carrying with it the value of the means of production used up and the value added by the expenditure of labor-
power in production. The third node, *commercial capital*, consists of
inventories of finished commodities awaiting sale. (Marx calls
commercial capital *commodity capital*.) When these commodities are
sold, the value in the circuit returns to the money form. Part of the
surplus value is consumed by capitalists and the State—partly in
the form of the payment of wages to unproductive labor—as we
shall see in Chapter 7. The recovery of the original costs together
with the unconsumed part of the surplus value returns to the
financial node, where it is available to finance another cycle of
production.

In highly developed capitalist economies the channels through which the unconsumed part of the surplus value returns to the circuit may be indirect. Part of the surplus value of one capital may be paid out in dividends or interest to capitalist households, which in turn lend it out to increase another capital, either directly or indirectly through a financial intermediary such as a bank. At the level of the circuit of social capital, the net effect is consumption of some of the surplus value and recommittal of some to the circuit of capital.

Each of the phases of this process take time. The production process, for example, requires a certain period—*the production lag*—between the time when labor-power and other inputs to production are purchased and the moment when the finished product emerges. It also takes some time for the commodity to find a buyer—*the realization lag*. In periods of crisis this latter lag may become much longer than normal, thereby reflecting the difficulty that capitalist firms have in finding buyers for the commodities produced. In addition, a *finance lag* separates the realization of value in the form of money and its recommittal to the production process in the form of capital advances. Marx calls these three lags the *turnover times* of the different phases of capitalist production.

Thus each of the nodes of the circuit of capital corresponds to a stock of value tied up in the form corresponding to that node; and between each of the nodes is a continuous flow of value moving from one form to the next. The flow between financial capital and productive capital is the flow of capital outlays. The flow between productive capital and commercial capital is the flow of finished commodities emerging from the production process. The flow between commercial capital and financial capital is the flow of sales of commodities.

The flow variables in the circuit of capital model correspond to the categories on the income or profit-and-loss statement of a capitalist firm. Capital outlays are the flow of costs of labor and nonlabor inputs to production over a period of time. The flow of sales is equal to the total sales of the firm (or group of firms) over some time period. The flow of finished commodities emerging from production corresponds to total production, that is, sales plus additions to inventories of finished commodities.

The stock variables in the circuit of capital model correspond to the categories on the asset side of the balance sheet of the firm. Financial capital is measured on the balance sheet as the financial assets of the firm: its holdings of cash, bank deposits, and debts from other firms and the State. Productive capital is the value of plant and equipment plus inventories of raw materials and partly finished goods. Commercial capital is the value of inventories of finished goods awaiting sale.

All the circuit of capital variables for a real capitalist firm or group of capitalist firms can be determined from ordinary accounting data. Indeed, it is striking that the ordinary conventions of capitalist accounting reflect the labor theory of value concepts so faithfully. This circumstance arises because both the labor theory of value and accounting practice insist on a strict rule of conservation of value except in production itself. For example, the value of productive capital has to be the sum of all past capital outlays less the sum of the values of all the finished products that have emerged from the production process. The wages paid to workers for work on partly finished products are allocated by accountants to the value of inventories of partly finished goods, in order to maintain this strict relation between stocks and flows of value.

A Model of the Circuit of Capital　　　　(Capital 2.7, 2.9, 2.12–2.14)

The circuit of capital consists of three flows of value—capital outlays, the value of finished product, and sales—and three stocks of value—productive capital, commercial capital, and financial (or money) capital. The flows of value in the circuit are governed by five parameters—the markup on costs (which in turn depends on the rate of surplus value and the composition of capital), the proportion of the surplus value recommitted to the circuit (which I shall call the *capitalization rate*), and the three time lags in the circuit, (the production lag, the realization lag, and the finance lag).

In constructing a mathematical representation of this circuit, we shall make the simplifying assumption that the time lags in the circuit are simple time delays. Hence, we assume that a dollar advanced as capital simply stays in the production process for a given time period and then emerges all at once as finished product. A more realistic, but mathematically more complicated, picture of time lags would allow for situations in which the value emerged from the production process gradually over time, some of it sooner and some later.

We shall use $C(t)$ to represent the flow of capital outlays at time

t, $P(t)$ to represent the flow of value of finished product (valued at cost), $S(t)$ to represent the flow of sales, $N(t)$ to represent the stock of productive capital, $X(t)$ to represent the stock of commercial capital (inventories of finished goods awaiting sale valued at cost), $F(t)$ to represent the stock of financial capital, p to represent the capitalization rate, q the markup on costs, T_P the time delay in production, T_R the time delay in selling the commodities, and T_F the time delay in reinvesting money capital. Thus $C(t)$ might be $1,000 billion capital advanced per year, $N(t)$ might be $3,000 billion tied up at a given moment in productive assets, q might be 50%, and T_P might be a 6-month time lag in production.

The equations of the model simply record the assumptions made about time lags and accounting conventions. Thus the flow of value of finished product at time t, $P(t)$, must be equal to the flow of capital outlays T_P periods earlier. We have

$$P(t) = C(t - T_P) \tag{5.2}$$

In a similar fashion, the flow of sales at time t corresponds to the flow of finished product T_R periods earlier, given the assumption that there is a fixed time lag in sales. Of course, the value of sales is larger than the value of finished product at cost because commodities are sold at prices that include surplus value or, to put it another way, because commodities are sold at prices that are marked up over costs.

$$S(t) = [1+q]P(t-T_R) \tag{5.3}$$

In a simple model that does not involve borrowing, new capital outlays must be financed from past sales. If we write $S'(t)$ for the part of sales that represents the recovery of the costs of production, and $S''(t)$ for the part of sales that represents the realization of surplus value, we have

$$S'(t) = P(t-T_R) = 1/[1+q]S(t) \tag{5.4a}$$
$$S''(t) = qP(t-T_R) = q/[1+q]S(t) \tag{5.4b}$$

and

$$C(t) = S'(t-T_F) + pS''(t-T_F) \tag{5.5}$$

because only the fraction p of the surplus value is assumed to be recommitted to the circuit of capital. The rest of surplus value is

consumed by capitalists or by the State or is used to support unproductive labor.

The accounting rules relating balance sheets and income statements then establish the laws that govern changes in the stocks of
value in the circuit of capital. For example, productive capital is
increased by capital outlays to purchase means of production and
labor-power and is decreased when finished product emerges from
the production process.

$$dN(t)/dt = C(t) - P(t) \tag{5.6}$$

In a similar fashion we can write down the laws governing the
evolution of the stocks of commercial capital and money capital.

$$dX(t)/dt = P(t) - S(t)/[1+q] = P(t) - S'(t) \tag{5.7}$$

$$\begin{aligned} dF(t)/dt &= S(t) - [1-p]S''(t) - C(t) \\ &= S'(t) + pS''(t) - C(t) \end{aligned} \tag{5.8}$$

Equations (5.2)–(5.8) constitute the basic model of the circuit of
capital.

Simple Reproduction in the Model *(Capital 2.18, 2.20)*

Intuitively we can see that one possible outcome of this system is
the smooth and balanced growth of all the stocks and flows at the
same geometric or exponential rate. Marx calls this pattern reproduction, and he examines it as a first step toward a full analysis of
accumulation. Accumulation itself would obey the same six equations, but the parameters p and q and the time lags would be
changing through time as a result of the accumulation process. For
example, the increase in the scale of production made possible by
accumulation might be reflected in changes in the rate of surplus
value (through technical change creating relative surplus value by
cheapening the cost of workers' subsistence) and in the composition of capital (because new techniques might require more means
of production in proportion to labor employed). As a result, q, the
markup on costs, would be changing as accumulation proceeds.
Models with constant parameters are much easier to analyze than
are models in which the parameters depend in a general way on
the process itself.

The simplest case to analyze is when $p = 0$, that is, when no
surplus value is accumulated and the capitalists consume their

whole income. Marx calls this case *simple reproduction*. In this case the capitalist economy continues unchanged in scale and proportions through time; and equations (5.2)–(5.5) become, by successive substitution,

$$P(t) = C(t - T_P) \tag{5.9}$$

$$S(t) = [1 + q]P(t - T_R) \tag{5.10}$$

$$S'(t) = P(t - T_R) = S(t)/[1 + q] \tag{5.11}$$

$$S''(t) = qP(t - T_R) = qC(t) \tag{5.12}$$

$$\begin{aligned} C(t) &= S'(t - T_F) = P(t - [T_R + T_F]) \\ &= C(t - [T_P + T_R + T_F]) \end{aligned} \tag{5.13}$$

$$C(t) = P(t) = S(t)/[1 + q] \tag{5.14}$$

Equations (5.9)–(5.14) show (as our intuition tells us they should) that if the capitalists consume all the surplus value, the flow of capital outlays will be constant from one time to another and the flow of value of finished output will also just be equal to this flow of capital outlays. The model cannot tell us how large these flows are; they will stay at whatever level they have when the process starts. Furthermore, the level of value of sales is just equal to the flow of value of finished output including the markup q. The capitalists consume the entire surplus value qP.

Equations (5.6)–(5.8) show that

$$dN/dt = C(t) - P(t) = 0$$

$$dX/dt = P(t) - S(t)/[1 + q] = 0$$

$$dF/dt = S(t) - [1 - p]S''(t) - C(t) = 0$$

Thus, the levels of the balance sheet stocks of value will remain unchanged over time as well. We can see how large these balance sheet items must be. Take, for example, $N(t)$, the stock of productive capital. It must be equal to $C(t)T_P$ because each dollar of capital outlays remains in the productive system for a time T_P. In a similar fashion we can see that

$$N(t) = C(t)T_P \tag{5.15}$$

$$X(t) = P(t)T_R = C(t)T_R \tag{5.16}$$

$$F(t) = S'(t)T_F = C(t)T_F \tag{5.17}$$

The stocks of value in the system must be just large enough to allow the flows to continue with the assumed time lags. For example, if $C(t)$ is $1,000 billion of capital advanced per year, and T_P is three years, we must have $N(t) = $3,000$ billion because it consists of the capital outlays paid out for the last three years.

These solutions also enable us to calculate the profit rate in simple reproduction. The profit rate r is the ratio of the surplus value (a flow) to the total capital tied up in production, or

$$r = \frac{S''(t)}{F(t) + N(t) + X(t)}$$

From the equations (5.9)–(5.17) we can calculate

$$r = \frac{qC(t)}{C(t)[T_F + T_p + T_R]} = \frac{q}{T_F + T_P + T_R} \tag{5.18}$$

Marx puts considerable weight on this formula. It says that the profit rate is equal to the markup, which determines how much each particle of value expands as it traverses the circuit of capital, divided by the total turnover time of capital, which tells how long it takes the particle to make the complete circuit.

Thus, for the case of simple reproduction, the circuit of capital model gives a complete picture of the flows and stocks of value and of the profit rate in a capitalist system.

Expanded Reproduction in the Circuit of Capital Model   (*Capital 2.21*)

To analyze expanded reproduction in the circuit of capital model, let us make the assumption that all the flows and stocks are increasing at the same, unknown, exponential rate g. Thus, for example, $C(t) = C(0)\exp(gt)$, where $\exp(\cdot)$ is the exponential function. In what follows we shall use several properties of the exponential function, especially

$$\exp(gt - gT) = \exp(g[t - T]) = \exp(gt)\exp(-gT) \tag{5.19}$$

$$\frac{d[\exp(gt)]}{dt} = g[\exp(gt)] \tag{5.20}$$

Equation (5.19) shows that when we look backward T periods along a path of exponential growth the size of the variable at that time, $t - T$, is just $\exp(-gT)$ times the size of the variable at time t. Equation (5.20) shows that the increase in an exponentially growing variable at any time is equal to the growth rate times the size of the variable at that time.

To begin with, we can simplify (5.2)–(5.5) by substitution. Putting (5.2) into (5.3) we get

$$S(t) = [1+q]C(t - [T_P + T_R]) \tag{5.21}$$

Because current sales depend on past production and because past production depends on capital outlays even further back, current sales depend on capital outlays in the past. The same reasoning leads to the conclusion that capital outlays themselves depend on their own past values (substitute (5.21) into (5.5)):

$$C(t) = [1+pq]C(t - [T_F + T_R + T_P]) \tag{5.22}$$

If $C(t)$ and all the other stock and flow variables are growing exponentially at the same, as yet unknown, rate g, then $C(t) = C(0)\exp(gt)$, where $C(0)$ is the size of the flow of capital outlays at time 0. Then (5.22) becomes

$$
\begin{aligned}
C(0)\exp(gt) &= [1+pq]C(0)\exp(g\{t - [T_F + T_R + T_P]\}) \tag{5.23} \\
&= C(0)\exp(gt)[1+pq]\exp(-g[T_F + T_R + T_P])
\end{aligned}
$$

We can divide through by $C(0)\exp(gt)$ to get the characteristic equation of this system:

$$1 = [1+pq]\exp(-g[T_F + T_R + T_P]) \tag{5.24}$$

or, multiplying both sides by $\exp(-g[T_F + T_R + T_P])$ and taking natural logarithms, we get

$$g = \frac{\ln(1+pq)}{T_F + T_R + T_P} \tag{5.25}$$

Equation (5.25) sums up a number of important insights about expanded reproduction in capitalist economies. It shows that the rate of expansion does indeed depend on the key parameters of the system: the markup q, which reflects the social relations of production and the development of forces of production as the product of the rate of surplus value and the composition of capital; p, the rate of capitalization of surplus value, which determines how much of the surplus value reenters the circuit of capital; and the time lags in the various phases of the circuit. The rate of expansion increases with the markup and capitalization rate and decreases with rises in any of the time lags. This equation thus provides a basic framework for the analysis of the political economy of accumulation in capitalist societies, because it shows the proximate variables that policy must affect in order to alter the rate of accumulation.

Equation (5.25) does not determine the size of the initial capital outlays, $C(0)$. This reflects the fact that the circuit of capital model depends only on the ratios of the key variables, under the hypothesis of reproduction, and not on their actual size. Thus a small economy would grow in exactly the same way as a large one if the two had the same basic parameters of accumulation. We can, for convenience, assume that $C(0) = 1$. Then we can use (5.2) and (5.3) to solve for $P(0)$ and $S(0)$.

$$P(0)\exp(gt) = C(0)\exp(g[t - T_P]) \tag{5.26a}$$
$$= \exp(gt)\exp(-gT_P), \quad \text{or}$$
$$P(0) = \exp(-gT_P) \tag{5.26b}$$
$$S(0) = [1+q]\exp(-g[T_P + T_R]) \tag{5.27a}$$
$$S'(0) = \exp(-g[T_P + T_R]) \tag{5.27b}$$
$$S''(0) = q\exp(-g[T_P + T_R]) \tag{5.27c}$$

It is also possible to solve (5.6)–(5.8) to find the sizes of the balance sheet asset categories—financial capital, productive capital, and commercial capital—given the hypothesis of expanded reproduction. For example, in expanded reproduction the stock of productive capital $N(t)$ must be growing steadily at the same rate as the rest of the system, g. Thus $N(t) = N(0)\exp(gt)$. This means that $dN(t)/dt = gN(t)$, by the second property of exponential growth functions (5.20). From (5.6) we have

$$dN(t)/dt = gN(0)\exp(gt) = C(t) - P(t) \tag{5.28a}$$
$$= \exp(gt)[1 - \exp(-gT_P)], \quad \text{or}$$
$$N(0) = [1 - \exp(-gT_P)]/g \tag{5.28b}$$

By exactly similar reasoning we can work out $X(0)$ and $F(0)$:

$$X(0) = \exp(-gT_P)[1 - \exp(-gT_R)]/g \tag{5.29}$$
$$F(0) = [1+pq]\exp(-g[T_P + T_R])[1 - \exp(-gT_F)]/g \tag{5.30}$$

These balance sheet quantities are all positive and depend on the rate of growth of the system and on the time lags, as we would expect.

Capitalists calculate the rate of profit as the ratio of the surplus value to the stock of capital tied up in their production. On a path of expanded reproduction we can calculate both the flow of realized surplus value and the stocks of capital tied up and thus explicitly calculate the profit rate for the whole system. This calculation obviously abstracts from the payment of interest, or of taxes out of surplus value, because it expresses the whole surplus value as a fraction of the capital tied up. The gross rate of profit, r, is

$$r = \frac{S''(t)}{F(t) + N(t) + X(t)} \tag{5.31}$$

On a path of expanded reproduction all the flows and stocks are growing at the same rate; hence $r(t)$ remains the same through time and is equal to

$$r = \frac{S''(0)}{F(0) + N(0) + X(0)} \tag{5.32}$$

From (5.27c) we see that $S''(0) = q\exp(-g[T_P + T_R])$. From (5.28b), (5.29), and (5.30), we can determine the total capital tied up at time 0:

$$F(0) + N(0) + X(0) = pq\exp(-g[T_P + T_R])/g \tag{5.33}$$

Thus we can solve (5.32) to get

$$r = \frac{g}{p} = \frac{\ln(1 + pq)}{p[T_P + T_R + T_F]} \tag{5.34}$$

Equation (5.34) shows that the profit rate is equal to the growth rate divided by the capitalization rate, or more directly, that the growth rate is the profit rate multiplied by the capitalization rate. This equation is sometimes known as the "Cambridge equation" and plays a major role in modern growth theory.

If we approximate $\ln(1 + pq)$ by pq, which is accurate as long as pq is not too large, we see that

$$r \cong \frac{q}{T_P + T_R + T_F} \tag{5.35}$$

This expression for the profit rate, which we have already seen in (5.18) is the one to which Marx usually refers.

Suppose, for example, that we are looking at a capitalist system in which the value of labor-power is 1/2 and consequently the rate of surplus value is 1 (100%) and in which the composition of capital is 1/3 and consequently the markup is also 1/3 (33.33%). If the time lags are 12 months in production, 6 months in sales, and 6 months in finance, the total time it takes a particle of value to traverse the circuit of capital is two years. If one-half the surplus value is reinvested in the circuit of capital, the growth rate g will equal $\ln(1.1667)/2 = 0.077$ (7.7%). The profit rate will be twice the growth rate, or 0.154 (15.4%), which is close to the markup divided by the total turnover time of capital.

Thus, for the case of expanded reproduction, the circuit of capital model gives a complete quantitative picture of capitalist accumulation.

Proportionality and Aggregate Demand
in Simple Reproduction   *(Capital 2.20)*

Marx raises, in Volume 2 of *Capital* (1893, chaps. 20, 21), the important question of what proportions of social capital must be allocated to different functions to sustain smooth reproduction. Marx retains the fundamental distinction characteristic of the labor theory of value between constant capital—produced inputs whose value is simply recovered in the value of the output—and variable capital—capital advanced to purchase labor-power that adds more than its own value to the value of the output. He proposes that for analytic purposes we divide the capitalist economy into two departments: Department I consists of all those activities that produce the elements of constant capital, that is, means of production; Department II consists of all those activities that produce means of subsistence for the reproduction of labor-power. These departments, however, are not the same thing as industries or sectors of the capitalist economy, for one industry or sector may contribute both to means of subsistence and to means of production. For instance, agriculture as a sector produces both food for reproduction of labor-power and raw materials for industry. The steel beams made in a mill may be used to build either a factory or an apartment house; and so on.

We can use the circuit of capital framework to study the problem of proportionality, both to gain insights into the conclusions Marx reaches and to generalize them. We shall write down the equations for the circuits of capital of Departments I and II separately and then specify, as Marx does, the necessary relations between them. First we shall take up the analysis of simple reproduction and then, in the next section, tackle the more complex mathematical issues involved in the analysis of expanded reproduction.

Each department can have its own markup, though I shall assume that the time delays in the two departments are the same. In the case of simple reproduction both departments have a capitalization rate equal to zero.

The basic model for Department I (Department II is exactly the same, but with the subscripts changed) is, using (5.2)–(5.5),

$$P_I(t) = C_I(t - T_P) \tag{5.36}$$
$$S_I(t) = [1 + q_1]P_I(t - T_R) \tag{5.37}$$
$$C_I(t) = S'_I(t - T_F) \tag{5.38}$$

In simple reproduction there is a necessary link between the production of each department and the social requirements for the output of that department. This is Marx's key insight into the requirements of proportionality in reproduction schemes. For example, the output of Department I is means of production, which must be bought in order to meet the productive requirements of the two departments. Department I's requirements for means of production in value terms are $[1 - k_I]C_I(t)$ because k_I is the proportion of capital outlays of Department I spent on variable capital; hence the rest must go to purchase constant capital, or means of production. Similarly, Department II's requirements for means of production are $[1 - k_{II}]C_{II}(t)$. These purchases correspond to the replacement of means of production used up in past cycles of production. In symbolic terms this relation can be expressed as

$$S_I(t) = [1 - k_I]C_I(t) + [1 - k_{II}]C_{II}(t) \tag{5.39}$$

A similar expression can be written down relating the sales of Department II to the wages paid in the two departments and to the surplus value, which by the assumption of simple reproduction is all consumed.

$$S_{II}(t) = k_I C_I(t) + k_{II} C_{II}(t) + S''_I(t) + S''_{II}(t) \tag{5.40}$$

This relation assumes that there is no time delay in spending of wages by workers or spending of their share of surplus value by capitalist households.

As long as there is no borrowing or lending outside the circuit of capital, the conservation of value assures us that if one of the two conditions (5.39) and (5.40) holds, the other one must hold as well.

In simple reproduction, we know that C_I remains constant through time. Thus we can write (5.39) as

$$S_I(t) = [1+q_I]C_I(t) = [1-k_I]C_I(t) + [1-k_{II}]C_{II}(t) \tag{5.41}$$

We can solve this equation for the proportion C_I/C_{II}, in which the social capital must be divided to allow for simple reproduction:

$$\frac{C_I}{C_{II}} = \frac{1-k_{II}}{q_I+k_I} \tag{5.42}$$

When we translate equation (5.42) back into Marx's notation, we see that it says that the sum of surplus value and variable capital in Department I must equal the constant capital in Department II. This principle is Marx's basic result in the analysis of simple reproduction. Department I reproduces its own constant capital; hence the rest of the value of its product, equal to its variable capital plus surplus value, must take the form of the constant capital necessary for Department II:

$$s_I + v_I = c_{II} \tag{5.43}$$

The significance of (5.42) in terms of Marx's scheme of simple reproduction is that, if the system begins with the capitals in the two departments in the proportions defined by (5.42), it can continue smoothly with no change in capital outlays or outputs. There will be just the right output from each department to allow production in the future to occur in the same quantities.

Intertwined with the analysis of the necessary proportions for reproduction in *Capital* (1893, chaps. 20 and 21) we find an investigation of the problem of aggregate demand. In his analysis of these schemes of reproduction Marx is trying to determine the sources of the money that realizes the commodities produced. The first insight that comes out of this investigation is that the money demand for the produced commodities arises directly or indirectly from the circuit of capital itself. This point is also the basis of Keynes's analysis of aggregate demand. The demand for produced commodities can be divided into three broad and exhaustive categories: the demand of capitals for means of production, the demand of workers for means of subsistence, and the demand of capitalist households (or of other households whose incomes arise from surplus value, or of the State) for means of subsistence or luxuries. In a closed capitalist system these are the only sources of money incomes and hence of money demand. Worker households and capitalist households and the State may have time delays in their spending of income, but ultimately they spend income that is derived from the circuit of capital itself.

To simplify the mathematical examples, we shall assume that there is no time delay in spending of wages by workers and that capitalist households have the same time delay, T_F, as capitalist firms have in spending their share of the surplus value. We also shall assume that luxury production is a part of Department II—to avoid the unnecessary multiplication of departments. Then we can write the aggregate money demand for commodities as

$$
\begin{aligned}
D(t) = {} & [1-k_I]C_I(t) + [1-k_{II}]C_{II}(t) \\
& + k_I C_I(t) + k_{II} C_{II}(t) \\
& + S''_I(t-T_F) + S''_{II}(t-T_F)
\end{aligned}
\tag{5.44}
$$

where the first line represents the demand of capitalist firms for means of production, the second the spending of wages by worker households, and the third the spending of surplus value by capitalist households.

The second important point in Marx's analysis is that the capital outlays of capitalist firms are themselves financed from past sales. This idea is expressed in the general circuit of capital model in equation (5.5) and in (5.38). Using this relation and the fact that the time delay in capitalist household spending is assumed to be the same as the time delay in capitalist firm spending, we can simplify (5.44) to

$$
D(t) = S_I(t-T_F) + S_{II}(t-T_F) = S(t-T_F)
\tag{5.45}
$$

Equation (5.45) expresses an extremely important insight. It shows that current demand depends on past sales, as long as capital outlays are assumed to be financed solely out of past sales. In the case of simple reproduction, this statement makes good sense. It means that the current aggregate demand is just large enough to realize all the produced commodities at the appropriate rate of sales to allow the reproduction process to continue. Of course, the lag in capitalist firm and household spending means that firms and households must hold reserves of money to finance their spending streams. In fact this reserve must be equal to $S(0)T_F$. In other words, the capitalists have to hold enough money balances to cover the period T_F between their receipt of sales revenues and their ability to spend it. Marx discovers this fact in his analysis in *Capital* (1893, chap. 20).

We can sum up Marx's analysis of simple reproduction in two statements. First, social capital must be allocated between the two departments in the appropriate proportions to allow reproduction to continue smoothly. Second, as long as the capitalists hold a sufficiently large fund of money balances, there is no difficulty in financing the aggregate demand required to realize all the commodities produced.

Proportionality in Expanded Reproduction   (*Capital* 2.21)

We now turn to the more complicated problems raised by expanded reproduction. The basic principles of the analysis are the same as for simple reproduction, but we now have to take account of the fact that the capitalization rates in the two departments will be positive rather than zero.

Each department can have its own markup and its own capitalization rate, although I shall continue to assume that the time delays in the two departments are the same. If the two departments are to expand at the same rate but have different markups and capitalization rates, it may be necessary for some of the capital accumulated in one department to be transferred to the other, because in general one department will accumulate more value than it needs for its expanded reproduction and the other less. In real capitalist economies this transfer could take place through lending and borrowing. Marx, however, abstracts from lending and borrowing at this stage of his analysis. Thus we shall simply assume that the markups and capitalization rates in the two departments are consistent with their expansion at the same rate without any transfers of capital between them, that is, we shall assume that each department finances its own expansion out of its own surplus value.

The basic model for Department I (Department II is exactly the same, but with the subscripts changed) is, just as in the case of simple reproduction,

$$P_{\mathrm{I}}(t) = C_{\mathrm{I}}(t - T_P) \tag{5.46}$$

$$S_{\mathrm{I}}(t) = [1 + q_{\mathrm{I}}]P_{\mathrm{I}}(t - T_R) \tag{5.47}$$

$$C_{\mathrm{I}}(t) = S_{\mathrm{I}}'(t - T_F) + p_{\mathrm{I}}S_{\mathrm{I}}''(t - T_F) \tag{5.48}$$

where $C_{\mathrm{I}}(t)$ is the flow of capital outlays for Department I, $P_{\mathrm{I}}(t)$ is the flow of finished product, and so on.

As in the case of simple reproduction, there is a necessary link between the production of each department and the social requirements for the output of that department. For example, the output of Department I is means of production, which must be bought in order to meet the productive requirements of the two departments. Department I's requirements for means of production in value terms are $[1 - k_{\mathrm{I}}]C_{\mathrm{I}}(t)$, because k_{I} is the proportion of capital outlays of Department I spent on variable capital and the rest must go to purchase constant capital, or means of production. These purchases correspond to the replacement of means of production used up in past cycles of production and to the expansion of means of production required by the expanded reproduction of the system. In symbolic terms this relation can be expressed, exactly as in the case of simple reproduction, as

$$S_{\mathrm{I}}(t) = [1 - k_{\mathrm{I}}]C_{\mathrm{I}}(t) + [1 - k_{\mathrm{II}}]C_{\mathrm{II}}(t) \tag{5.49}$$

A similar relation can be written down relating the sales of Department II to the wages paid in the two departments and the part of the surplus value consumed:

$$S_{\mathrm{II}}(t) = k_{\mathrm{I}}C_{\mathrm{I}}(t) + k_{\mathrm{II}}C_{\mathrm{II}}(t) + [1 - p_{\mathrm{I}}]S_{\mathrm{I}}''(t) + [1 - p_{\mathrm{II}}]S_{\mathrm{II}}''(t) \tag{5.50}$$

This relation assumes that there is no time delay in spending of wages by workers or spending of their share of surplus value by capitalist households. As long as there is no borrowing or lending outside the circuit of capital, the conservation of value assures us that if one of the two conditions (5.49) or (5.50) holds, the other one must hold as well.

Successive substitution in equations (5.46)–(5.48) yields

$$S_I(t) = [1 + p_I q_I] S_I(t - [T_P + T_R + T_F]) \tag{5.51a}$$

$$S_{II}(t) = [1 + p_{II} q_{II}] S_{II}(t - [T_P + T_R + T_F]) \tag{5.51b}$$

If each department is undergoing expanded reproduction at the rate g, so that $S_I(t) = S_I(0)\exp(gt)$—and likewise for Department II—then by the same methods we used to solve the aggregate circuit of capital model we can see that

$$g = \frac{\ln(1 + p_I q_I)}{T_P + T_R + T_F} = \frac{\ln(1 + p_{II} q_{II})}{T_P + T_R + T_F} \tag{5.52}$$

We shall assume that p, q, and the time delays for the two departments are compatible with this relationship. If the time delays are the same in the two departments, then $p_I q_I = p_{II} q_{II}$. If the economy is on a path of balanced expanded reproduction growing at rate g, then the same relations between the size of the sales flows and the size of the capital outlay flows must hold in each department as held for the economy as a whole (see the section *Expanded Reproduction in the Circuit of Capital Model*):

$$S_I(0) = [1 + q_I] C_I(0)\exp(-g[T_P + T_R + T_F]) \tag{5.53a}$$

$$S_{II}(0) = [1 + q_{II}] C_{II}(0)\exp(-g[T_P + T_R + T_F]) \tag{5.53b}$$

On a path of expanded reproduction, equation (5.49)—the proportionality condition for expanded reproduction—becomes

$$S_I(0) = [1 - k_I] C_I(0) + [1 - k_{II}] C_{II}(0) \tag{5.54}$$

or, using (5.53),

$$(1 + q_I) C_I(t - [T_P + T_R + T_F]) = [1 - k_I] C_I(t) + [1 - k_{II}] C_{II}(t) \tag{5.55}$$

We can solve (5.55) for the general proportionality condition for expanded reproduction, which is the foundation of Marx's results in *Capital* (1893, chap. 21).

$$\frac{C_I(0)}{C_{II}(0)} = \frac{[1 - k_{II}]\exp(g[T_P + T_R])}{[1 + q_I] + [1 - k_I]\exp(g[T_P + T_R])} \tag{5.56}$$

In the case of simple reproduction, $g = 0$ because $p_I = p_{II} = 0$ and equation (5.56) reduces to equation (5.42), which we have already seen.

But equation (5.56) also specifies the proportions needed to maintain expanded reproduction in both departments and can help us resolve a problem that nagged Marx.

Marx implicitly treats the problem of expanded reproduction as a period model, with periods that he refers to as "years." Capital outlays take place at the beginning of a year, and production is completed within the year. The product is realized at the beginning of the next year by the sale of the output. In the notation that we have been using, for Department I $C_I(t)$ is capital outlays at the beginning of year t, $P_I(t)$ is the flow of finished product at the end of year t, and $S_I(t)$ is the sales at the beginning of year t; similar notation is used for Department II. Marx's assumptions in working out his schema of reproduction are

$$P(t) = C(t) \tag{5.57}$$

$$S(t) = [1+q]P(t-1) \tag{5.58}$$

$$C(t) = S'(t) + pS''(t) \tag{5.59}$$

for each department. The balance condition he proposes is that the output of Department I be realized through the capital outlays for constant capital in the two departments.

$$S_I(t) = [1-k_I]C_I(t) + [1-k_{II}]C_{II}(t) \tag{5.60}$$

Marx's system is a set of difference equations, but a comparison of equations (5.57)–(5.60) with equations (5.46)–(5.49) shows that they are exactly the same as the circuit of capital equations, with $T_P = T_F = 0$ and $T_R = 1$. Thus (5.56) also gives the necessary initial conditions for balanced growth in Marx's schemas. Because in Marx's model $[1+pq] = \exp(g)$ (for either department), we can write (5.56) as

$$\frac{C_I(0)}{C_{II}(0)} = \frac{[1-k_{II}][1+p_Iq_I]}{[1+q_I]+[1+k_I][1+p_Iq_I]} \tag{5.61}$$

The significance of (5.61) in terms of Marx's schemas is simple. If we start with the capitals in the two departments in the proportions indicated by (5.61), it is possible for the system to continue smoothly along a path of balanced expanded reproduction. If we start with any other proportions, it is impossible to meet all the conditions for expanded reproduction.

For example, consider Marx's first attempt to develop a consistent schema of expanded reproduction (1893, pp. 505–521). He sets up the following tableau, in arbitrary units of value:

	c	v	s	$c+v+s$
I	4,000	1,000	1,000	6,000
II	1,500	376	376	2,252

Marx assumes that each department converts half its surplus value into capital; hence, in the circuit of capital notation, $p_I = p_{II} = 1/2$. He apparently wants to have the same composition of capital $k_I = k_{II} = 0.2$ in both departments, although to achieve this the variable capital and surplus value in Department II ought to be 375, not 376. The rate of exploitation is the same, 1, in each department; hence they have the same markups, $q_I = q_{II} = 0.2$.

If we follow Marx in tracing the consequences of these assumptions, we find that the demand for the output of Department I consists of the replacement of its own constant capital, the replacement of Department II's constant capital, and the provision of additional constant capital to allow each department to expand its operations in the original proportions. This demand is equal to 6,050:

c_I	$+ c_{II}$	$+ p_I[1-k_I]s_I$	$+ p_{II}[1-k_{II}]s_{II}$
4,000	+ 1,500	+ 400	+ 150

which is 50 more than the actual output of Department I in the tableau. A similar calculation shows that the demand for the output of Department II is 50 too small. The discrepancy annoyed Marx, and he devoted several pages of his notes to the attempt to find a schema that would exhibit proportional expanded reproduction.

The source of the discrepancy can be found in equation (5.61). When we use the parameters assumed by Marx in equation (5.61), we can see that the ratio of C_I to C_{II} needed to achieve balanced expanded reproduction is 2.75. Marx's initial ratio, however, is $5,000/1875 = 2.6667$. If Marx had started with a capital of 1818.18 in Department II, instead of 1875, he would have found that the balancing conditions were satisfied.

One central insight of Marx's study of expanded reproduction is that the expansion of a capitalist economy requires an appropriate division of the social capital between the production of means of subsistence and the production of further means of production.

The proportions required depend on the basic parameters of accumulation in the two departments, the compositions of capital, rates of surplus value, rates of capitalization of surplus value, and time lags in the phases of the circuit of capital. Marx poses this problem clearly and uses numerical examples to illustrate the solutions for simple reproduction. We have seen here that a consistent extension of his ideas enables us to give a general solution to the problem of proportionality and thus to complete the argument Marx left incomplete in Volume 2 of *Capital*.

Aggregate Demand in Expanded Reproduction

Generalization of the analysis of the section *Proportionality and Aggregate Demand in Simple Reproduction* provides an approach to the problem of aggregate demand in the case of expanded reproduction. To simplify the mathematical examples, we shall continue to assume that there is no time delay in spending of wages by workers and that capitalist households have the same time delay, T_F, as capitalist firms in spending their share of the surplus value. We also shall assume that luxury production is a part of Department II, to avoid the unnecessary multiplication of departments. Then we can write the aggregate money demand for commodities as

$$
\begin{aligned}
D(t) = &\; [1-k_I]C_I(t) + [1-k_{II}]C_{II}(t) \\
&+ k_I C_I(t) + k_{II}C_{II}(t) \\
&+ [1-p_I]S_I''(t-T_F) + [1-p_{II}]S_{II}''(t-T_F)
\end{aligned}
\tag{5.62}
$$

where the first line represents the demand of capitalist firms for means of production, the second the spending of wages by worker households, and the third the spending of surplus values by capitalist households.

As in the case of simple reproduction, capital outlays of capitalist firms are themselves financed from past sales. This idea is expressed in the general circuit of capital model in equations (5.5) and (5.38). Using this relation and the fact that the time delay in capitalist household spending is assumed to be the same as the time delay in capitalist firm spending, we can simplify (5.62) to

$$
D(t) = S_I(t-T_F) + S_{II}(t-T_F) = S(t-T_F)
\tag{5.63}
$$

Equation (5.62) shows that current demand depends on past sales, as long as capital outlays are assumed to be financed solely out of past sales. If we assume that the system is on a path of expanded reproduction at rate g, then we find that

$$D(t) = D(0)\exp(gt) = S(t - T_F) \tag{5.64}$$
$$= S(0)\exp(gt)\exp(-gT_F)$$
$$= S(t)\exp(-gT_F)$$

In the case of simple reproduction, when $g = 0$, equation (5.64) creates no puzzles. It says that the current aggregate demand is just large enough to realize all the produced commodities at the appropriate rate of sales to enable the reproduction process to continue. As we have seen, the lag in capitalist firm and household spending means that firms and households must hold reserves of money equal to $S(0)T_F$ to finance their spending streams.

But in the case of expanded reproduction, when $g > 0$, equation (5.64) seems to create a paradox because it shows that the aggregate money demand for produced commodities is smaller than the amount required to maintain smooth expanded reproduction. This difference will exist as long as both g and T_F are greater than zero. Furthermore, the difference between demand and realization grows as the system expands; hence the solution of having capitalists start with a money reserve, which worked for simple reproduction, will not work for expanded reproduction. Any finite initial reserve of money would be exhausted at some point on the path of expanded reproduction.

This paradox attracted the attention of later Marxist writers, notably Rosa Luxemburg (1913), who based her analysis of imperialism on it. She argued that a closed capitalist system undergoing accumulation would always run into inadequacies of aggregate demand and as a consequence would be forced to seek external markets to realize its surplus production. Although Luxemburg is correct in pointing to the difference between aggregate demand and necessary realization that is inherent in Marx's setup, her solution is not convincing. Where do the external markets get the money to buy the surplus product of the capitalist system? If they get it by selling something (labor-power or raw materials) to the capitalist system, they add as much to the value of the commodities that need to be realized as they do to the demand for them and thus do not diminish the demand gap. If they are supposed to hold large stocks of gold, which they spend on capitalist commodities, the same problem arises as in the closed system, namely, that with continuous expanded reproduction any finite stock of gold will be exhausted in a finite time. Luxemburg herself recognized this problem in her treatment of specific examples of imperialism, where she makes clear that the source of the money spent by imperialized countries to buy capitalist products is, in fact, loans from the capitalist system itself. This critique, of course, does not rule out the idea that capitalism systematically gives rise to imperialism through other mechanisms, such as the competition of capitals for access to protected markets, to labor-power, or to important sources of raw materials, or the pressure created by declining profit opportunities to open up new fields of investment of capital.

Because real capitalist economies do succeed in maintaining continuous accumulation without always running into problems of inadequate demand, there clearly must be general methods of resolving the paradox expressed in equation (5.64). Marx himself, at the very end of Volume 2 of *Capital* (1893, pp. 522–523), proposes one solution, which is taken up by Bukharin (1972) in his critique of Rosa Luxemburg. Marx points out that it is not true that all the commodities produced have to be realized by being exchanged against money. The money-commodity gold, once produced, is already value in the money form and thus does not need to be sold. If one posits a gold-producing sector of exactly the right size, namely, with production exactly equal to the difference between money demand and realization expressed in equation (5.64), then the problem of realization is solved. The money demand on the right-hand side of (5.64) is sufficient to realize all the nonmoney commodities, and the rest of commodity production is gold, which does not need to be realized. The gold-producing sector must grow at the same rate as the rest of the system in order to maintain this balance. Of course, any improvements in financial methods that shorten T_F will reduce the required size of the gold-producing sector.

In modern capitalist economies gold production plays a very small role, and the links between money and gold have become very weak. The other way to resolve the paradox of equation (5.64) is to relax the assumption that current capital outlays are financed entirely from past sales. If some capital outlays are financed by borrowing against the prospect of future sales, then the realization gap can be closed. This requires the alteration of (5.64) to

$$C(t) = S'(t - T_F) + pS''(t - T_F) + B(t) \tag{5.65}$$

where $B(t)$ is new capitalist borrowing. If we use (5.65) in calculating the aggregate demand for the system, we get

$$D(t) = S(t - T_F) + B(t) \tag{5.66}$$

We see that new borrowing by the capitalists to finance capital outlays can close the gap between demand financed by past sales and the level of demand required to maintain reproduction. In fact, borrowing by capitalist households, or by the State, can also close the gap. The sustainable rate of growth of the system obviously depends on the level of such new borrowing: the higher the total borrowing, the faster the rate of expanded reproduction that can be achieved by the system.

This investigation is important because it establishes a fundamental link between credit and the conditions for the expanded reproduction of the capitalist system. It suggests that in a crisis, when aggregate demand is inadequate, the failure to meet the conditions for expanded reproduction will be connected to changes in the expansion of credit.

We can go no further on the basis of the narrow assumptions of reproduction. We can see that there are necessary links between the parameters of the accumulation process and credit (or gold production) but the directions of causality in the system are hidden by the assumption that it is somehow achieving fully balanced reproduction.

Conclusion

Volume 2 of *Capital* develops a formal model of the capitalist system as a whole through the analysis of the circuit of capital. We have used this concept to construct a mathematical analysis of simple and expanded reproduction in a circuit of capital model. We see that the social relations and development of productive forces in a capitalist system, as reflected in the rate of surplus value, the composition of capital, the time delays in the phases of the circuit of capital, and the rate of capitalization of surplus value, determine the rate of expansion that can be sustained by the system. It is striking that these determinations do not directly involve the availability of labor-power or of raw materials for production.

Of course, shortages of labor-power may push up wages and thus reduce the rate of surplus value, just as shortages of raw materials may raise the cost of raw material inputs to production and lower the composition of capital. But capital still faces internal limits to its drive for expansion.

6

The Equalization of the Rate of Profit

The Rate of Profit   *(Capital 3.1–3.4)*

The fundamental point of Marx's analysis of capitalist production is that surplus value has its origin in unpaid labor. Marx believed, however, that the participants in capitalist economic relations have difficulty in perceiving this fact. Commodity relations tend to obscure the social reality that supports them, and consequently the origin of surplus value is not apparent without critical and theoretical effort. When a worker sells her labor-power to the capitalist at its value, for example, she is not directly conscious of the surplus labor she performs. Only by considering the ensemble of social relations as a whole can the worker perceive that capitalists as a class are appropriating surplus labor from workers as a class.

The same problem of perspective afflicts capitalists as well. The capitalist is concerned proximately with the expansion of her capital because the capital appears immediately as self-expanding value. Thus surplus value appears to the capitalist as an increment to the capital already advanced. The origin of surplus value in the exploitation of workers is thus abstract and irrelevant to the individual capitalist.

In quantitative terms the mystification of the origin of surplus value is achieved by expressing surplus value as a fraction of the total capital advanced (or tied up) in production rather than as a fraction of variable capital, as in the rate of surplus value. This ratio is called the *rate of profit*. In real capitalist economies capitalists face many deductions from their surplus value: the payment of wages for unproductive labor for sales and administrative expense, rent, interest, and taxes (Chapter 7). For the moment, we shall ignore these different forms of surplus value and look only at the ratio of total surplus value to total capital invested, understanding that this is a larger measure of surplus value than those usually employed by capitalists in calculating a rate of profit. (This measure would be the conventional rate of profit if none of these deductions existed.)

If we write K for the total value tied up in the production process, the rate of profit r is

$$r = \frac{s}{K} = \left[\frac{s}{v}\right]\left[\frac{v}{v+c}\right]\left[\frac{c}{K}\right] \tag{6.1}$$

or

$$r = ekn = qn \tag{6.2}$$

where $e = s/v$ is the rate of surplus value or the rate of exploitation, $k = v/[v+c]$ is the composition of capital, and $n = [v+c]/K$ is the *rate of turnover of capital*, that is, the ratio of the flow of capital advanced to the stock of capital tied up in the production circuit. In the circuit of capital model, $n = 1/[T_P+T_R+T_F]$ exactly in simple reproduction, and approximately in expanded reproduction, as we have seen in Chapter 5.

The rate of profit relates the surplus value to the whole capital advanced to appropriate it. In this expression the real social origin of the surplus value according to the labor theory of value is blurred. First, the distinction between variable capital and constant capital is obliterated because the markup is calculated on the basis of the total costs of the capitalist, without distinguishing labor costs from nonlabor costs. Second, the introduction of the rate of turnover relates the surplus value to the total capital invested, not just to that part of the capital that actually emerges in the finished product in the period.

The theory of the origin of profit is the basis of explanations of the rate of profit and its changes. The decomposition of the rate of profit in equation (6.1) suggests a method of analysis because any changes in the rate of profit must act through changes in the rate of surplus value, the composition of capital, or the rate of turnover of capital. This contrasts with, for example, the explanation of the rate of profit in neoclassical economics as the marginal product of capital, or the scarcity price of capital, or the intertemporal equilibrium relative price of present and future goods.

The Equalization of the Rate of Profit   *(Capital 3.8–3.10)*

Proponents of both neoclassical and Marxist economic theory agree that there is a tendency for profit rates in different sectors of the capitalist economy to be equalized by the competition between capitals. The simplest rationale for this idea is the notion that capital will move from sectors where profit rates are low to sectors where profit rates are high. This movement reduces the pressure of sales competition in those sectors where profit rates are low and allows prices of outputs in those sectors to rise, thus raising the gross profit and the profit rate. Symmetrically, the movement of capital to sectors with high profit rates increases the pressure of sales competition in those sectors and tends to force profits and profit rates down. This process will tend to push profit rates toward equality in the various sectors.

The notion of equal profit rates must be analyzed at the appropriate level. The theories mentioned above do not argue that we should expect to see the same profit rates across sectors at every instant in a real economy. Changes in technology, demand, and resource availability will constantly be altering the cost structures of different sectors and thus will constantly be creating differences in profit rates. The competition among capitals just as constantly tends to erode these differences and produce uniformity of the profit rate. Furthermore, the theory of competition among capitals is subject to qualification as we reduce the level of abstraction. If there are barriers to the free mobility of capital, obviously the process of equalization cannot work. Thus if some capitals have advantages due to the scale of production or to access to some technology that can be kept secret from potential competitors or to protection by legislation, the tendency of capital mobility to equalize profit rates may be frustrated, even for a very long time. These possibilities do not contradict the tendency for the profit rate to be equalized because they represent qualifications of the general tendency.

It is not even necessary to believe that capital actually moves between sectors in order to motivate equalization of the rate of profit. The *threat* of capital mobility may be enough to force prices and profit rates down in high profit rate sectors, even when no capital actually moves from other sectors to them.

Economic theorists generally agree on the relevance of models of economies in which profit rates have actually achieved equality across sectors. These models are motivated on a variety of grounds. First, if the adjustment process is rapid, actual economies would exhibit profit rates in different sectors that are very nearly equal to one another, and the model of exact equality might be a good approximation. Second, even if actual economies are subject to large shocks and have important barriers to the mobility of capital, the study of models in which profit rates are equalized is a good logical test of the consistency of the economic theory being developed. Third, if a theory can successfully deal with the situation in which profit rates are equalized, then there is a good chance that it can deal with failures of competition if it is appropriately modified to take into account the specific limits on competition that are important in the real economy.

There is another, more abstract and Hegelian, rationale for studying economies in which profit rates are equalized. Capital appears phenomenally as self-expanding value. (Of course, the labor theory of value argues that the secret of this self-expansion is simply the exploitation of workers.) Thus the simplest determination of capital is just its rate of self-expansion, or of potential self-expansion—which is the profit rate. Because we want to begin to study an ensemble of capitals, it is natural to start with the assumption that they are all alike in this basic determination, that is, that they all have the same profit rate. This is the first step toward a complete analysis in which we would introduce those particular features that differentiate capitals from one another and lead to differences in their potential rates of self-expansion, features such as the unevenness of technical change, monopoly, and legislative barriers to competition.

Incompatibility of Equal Exchange and Equal Profit Rates
(Capital 3.8)

Under conditions of equal exchange, that is, when the money price of each produced commodity is equal to the social labor directly and indirectly embodied in the commodity divided by the value of money, the value added in every sector is proportional to the living labor time expended in that sector. If the wage is equal across sectors, then the rates of surplus value will be the same in all sectors and the amount of surplus value produced and realized in a sector will be proportional to the labor time expended in that sector. But the amount of capital tied up per unit of labor time expended may not be the same in each sector. If it is not—and there is no good theoretical or empirical reason to think that it is— the ratios of surplus value in a sector to capital invested in the sector, that is, the profit rates, will differ between sectors. Thus the assumptions of the labor theory of value and of equal ex- change are inconsistent with the achievement of equal profit rates across sectors, as Marx clearly knew when he wrote the chapters in Volume 3 of *Capital* on the equalization of profit rates (before he published Volume 1).

A very simple model of an economy that has two sectors— wheat and steel—can be used to illustrate this point. The produc- tion of a unit of wheat at the end of a period requires inputs of 1 unit of labor and 1/4 unit of steel at the beginning of the period. The production of a unit of steel at the end of a period requires inputs of 1 unit of labor and 1/2 unit of steel at the beginning of the period. The capital tied up is equal to the wages of the workers and the cost of the steel input. We can summarize this technology in an input–output table:

	Input			
Product	Wheat	Steel	Labor	Output
Wheat	0	1/4	1	1
Steel	0	1/2	1	1

How much labor is directly and indirectly embodied in a unit of steel? If v_s is the labor value of a unit of steel, it must satisfy the equation

$$v_s = 1 + [1/2]v_s \tag{6.3}$$

because there is 1 unit of direct labor in the unit of steel, plus the labor embodied in 1/2 unit of steel. Similarly, the labor value of a unit of wheat, v_w, must satisfy the equation

$$v_w = 1 + [1/4]v_s \tag{6.4}$$

These two equations can be solved easily (in fact, equation (6.3) can be solved by itself), and the labor values are $v_s = 2$, $v_w = 3/2$. If the value of money is 1, that is, \$1 is the value added created by one unit of labor, then the prices of wheat and steel under conditions of equal exchange would be $p_s = \$2.00$, $p_w = \$1.50$. The value added in a unit of steel is just \$1.00, as is the value added in a unit of wheat.

Suppose that the wage is \$.50 per unit of labor-power and that 1 unit of labor-power corresponds to 1 unit of labor time actually expended. Then the surplus value per unit of steel will be \$.50, and the surplus value per unit of wheat will be \$.50 as well. The capital tied up per unit of steel, however, is \$1.50 (\$1.00 corresponding to the 1/2 unit of steel bought at the beginning of the period and \$.50 corresponding to the wages paid to the worker at the beginning of the period), whereas the capital tied up in producing a unit of wheat is \$1.00 (\$.50 corresponding to the 1/4 unit of steel bought at the beginning of the period and \$.50 corresponding to the wages paid to the worker at the beginning of the period). The profit rate in steel production at these prices is thus $1/3 = \$.50/\$1.50 = 33.33\%$, whereas the profit rate in wheat production is $1/2 = \$.50/\$1.00 = 50\%$.

This result is generally true. Unless the value of the capital invested per worker is the same across sectors, then if prices correspond to equal exchange and wage rates are the same in different sectors, profit rates will not be the same. Of course, in real economies wage rates are not uniform across sectors; but there is no reason to think that the actual differences (due to differences in the skill or bargaining position of workers in different sectors) will be related to the amount of capital per unit labor tied up in each sector. Thus these real differences in wage rates will not help to equalize the rates of profit.

We can express this model in terms of a tableau like the ones Marx employs in *Capital* (1894, pp. 155–157). Suppose the economy produces 10,000 units of steel and 10,000 units of wheat. We would find the following relations:

Sector	c	v	s	c+v+s	p	s/v	r(%)
Wheat	5,000	5,000	5,000	15,000	\$1.50	1	50.00
Steel	10,000	5,000	5,000	20,000	\$2.00	1	33.33
Total	15,000	10,000	10,000	35,000		1	40.00

The problem (which is often called the *transformation problem*) is to explain how the equalization of the profit rate is compatible with the labor theory of value.

Marx's Method   (Capital 3.9)

Marx argues that the equalization of rates of profit is compatible with the labor theory of value if we give up the postulate of equal exchange and allow money prices of commodities to be higher or lower than the amount of labor directly and indirectly embodied in the commodities. The labor theory of value continues to be valid in the sense that the aggregate value added in the economy as a whole is an expression of the total social labor time. The prices that equalize the rate of profit across sectors Marx calls *prices of production*.

In the example developed in the preceding section Marx's method would work as follows. The profit rate in steel production is below the average, whereas the profit rate in wheat production is above the average. Thus the price of wheat must fall and the price of steel must rise. Marx argues that these price changes merely redistribute the surplus value between the two sectors. In fact, if we were able to move $1,000 of surplus value from the wheat sector to the steel sector we would find, holding constant capital and variable capital unchanged in each sector, that the profit rates would become equal. The new tableau looks like this:

Sector	c	v	s	c+v+s	p	s/v	r(%)
Wheat	5,000	5,000	4,000	14,000	$1.40	1 (0.8)	40.00
Steel	10,000	5,000	6,000	21,000	$2.10	1 (1.2)	40.00
Total	15,000	10,000	10,000	35,000		1	40.00

The new prices of wheat and steel are calculated by dividing the total sales price ($14,000 in the case of wheat) by the output (10,000) to get the unit price. Marx argues that the price of wheat will fall to $1.40 and the price of steel will rise to $2.10 as a result of the competition of capitals. The value of money remains the same; consequently the price of wheat is below its value (the price corresponds to 1.4 units of labor being embodied in a unit of wheat, whereas in reality 1.5 units of labor are embodied) and the price of steel is above its value. The rates of surplus value produced in each sector have not changed, but the apparent rates of surplus value realized in each sector have changed (these apparent rates are noted in parentheses).

Furthermore, Marx argues, the redistribution of surplus value has no effect on the aggregate flows of value; hence the labor theory of value continues to hold exactly for the economy as a whole. His method for finding prices of production holds constant (1) total value added, total surplus value, total variable capital, and the social rate of surplus value; (2) constant capital, and the total sales price for the economy as a whole; and (3) the average profit rate for the economy as a whole.

Marx claimed that this method was general and that it was possible to calculate prices of production that equalized the rate of profit while maintaining all of the results of the labor theory of value for the economy in the aggregate.

If this method were acceptable, it would indeed be a powerful demonstration of the compatibility of the labor theory of value with the principle of the equalization of the rate of profit. In fact, the labor theory of value would be compatible with any pricing rule, even one that did not equalize rates of profit, because it took into account technical change, monopoly, or state intervention.

The Defect in Marx's Method   (Capital 3.9)

When Volume 2 of *Capital* was published, Engels included an introduction in which he challenged non-Marxist economists to solve the problem of consistency of the labor theory of value with the principle of equalization of the rate of profit (which was, indeed, a leading problem in the development of Ricardian economic theory). Engels claimed that Marx had explained the relation of these principles and that his success proved the superiority of his methods over those of non-Marxist economists even in attacking issues raised by non-Marxist research programs. This somewhat macho gesture on Engels' part ensured that withering hostile critical attention would be directed to Marx's solution when Engels published Volume 3 of *Capital*.

What the critics immediately pointed out was that Marx's method is inconsistent because the final tableau assumes that, in our example, steel sells at a price of $2.10 but producers buy steel at the original equal exchange price of $2.00. If the price of steel were

$2.10, the 2,500 units of steel required to produce 10,000 units of wheat would cost $5,250, not $5,000, and the 5,000 units of steel required by the steel sector as an input would cost $10,500. With just this adjustment, the tableau would be

Sector	c	v	s	c+v+s	p	s/v	r(%)
Wheat	5,250	5,000	3,750	14,000	$1.40	1 (0.75)	36.59
Steel	10,500	5,000	5,500	21,000	$2.10	1 (1.1)	35.48
Total	15,750	10,000	9,250	35,000		0.925	35.92

But in this tableau profit rates in the two sectors are not equalized. Furthermore, the social rate of surplus value and the social profit rate have both changed, as has the value added and hence the value of money.

This criticism of Marx's method has been generally accepted as a valid one. But some people have gone further and have argued that Marx also treats variable capital inconsistently. In the original (equal exchange) tableau, the money wage was $.50 and the price of wheat was $1.50. If we assume for a moment that workers spend their wages only on wheat, this implies a real wage of 1/3 unit of wheat per unit of labor-power. But in Marx's proposed solution the price of wheat has fallen to $1.40. If the money wage remained at $.50, the real wage would have risen to 0.357 units of wheat per unit of labor-power. These critics put great weight on Marx's statement in *Capital* (1867, pp. 170–171) that the value of labor-power is the labor time required to produce the means of subsistence necessary to reproduce labor-power. If 1/3 unit of wheat is necessary to reproduce a unit of labor-power before the transformation, these people argue, is it not still necessary after the transformation, and should not Marx have adjusted the real wage downward to $.4667 (which would buy 1/3 unit of wheat when the price of wheat is $1.40)? This would require a further adjustment in the tableau by altering the value of variable capital as well as the value of constant capital.

This second criticism has not been universally accepted as valid because the value of labor-power can be interpreted, as we have seen earlier, either as the value of money multiplied by the money wage or as the labor embodied in the commodities workers actually consume. These two interpretations are equivalent under the assumption of equal exchange, but it is precisely the assumption

of equal exchange that has been dropped in dealing with the transformation problem. If we hold to the first definition of the value of
labor-power, which interprets this as the amount of abstract social
labor workers receive in the form of wages in return for a unit of
labor-power, then we need not make the second adjustment of
variable capital in the transformation tableaux. What we need to
do is to hold the value of money and the money wage constant.
Marx's method does this, but, as we have seen, when we introduce the output prices as the prices of constant capital, the value
of money changes.

It is possible to apply Marx's method iteratively—by repeating
the transformation procedure over and over again until the prices
and profit rates converge (Shaikh, 1977). The characteristics of the
final tableau will depend on exactly how this iteration is carried
out and exactly what quantities are kept constant in each of the
iterations. The solution can also be reached by writing down the
conditions the prices and profit rate have to meet and solving the
resulting equations.

Completing Marx's Approach

Let us first show that Marx's method can be followed in a manner
consistent with Marx's idea that surplus value is merely redistributed in the transformation process. This approach requires that
we hold the value of money and the value of labor-power (in the
sense of the money wage multiplied by the value of money) constant in the transformation.

In terms of the example we have been following, the final prices
and profit rate r have to satisfy these equations:

$$p_s = [1+r]([1/2]p_s + 1/2) \tag{6.5}$$

$$p_w = [1+r]([1/4]p_s + 1/2) \tag{6.6}$$

$$10,000(p_s - [1/2]p_s) + 10,000(p_w - [1/4]p_s) = 20,000 \tag{6.7}$$

The first two equations require that the profit rate in the two
sectors be the same, given the wage rate of 1/2; and the third
equation requires that the value added remain the same (a con-
straint that will keep the value of money constant). The solutions
for these equations are $p_s = \$2.2078$, $p_w = \$1.4480$, and $r = 37.65\%$. The final tableau is

Sector	c	v	s	c+v+s	p	s/v	r(%)
Wheat	5,520	5,000	3,960	14,480	$1.448	1 (0.79)	37.65
Steel	11,040	5,000	6,040	22,080	$2.208	1 (1.21)	37.65
Total	16,560	10,000	10,000	36,560		1	37.65

It is possible to use this approach for any number of commodities and any structure of input–output coefficients. Notice that the first set of claims Marx makes for his method are all met: value added, surplus value, and the rate of surplus value are unchanged from the initial equal exchange tableau. The other two sets of claims, however, are not satisfied in this approach. The value of constant capital has not remained unchanged, and as a result the total price of the commodities has changed and the final social profit rate, 37.65%, is not the same as the original equal exchange social profit rate of 40%. The final tableau is compatible with the basic claims of the labor theory of value in the sense that the total value added in the system corresponds to the total social labor time and the surplus value in the system corresponds to the unpaid labor of the workers. The surplus value has, in fact, merely been redistributed by unequal exchange.

It is true that the real wage has risen. If we assume that workers consume only wheat, then the money wage of $.50 now buys 0.345 unit of wheat instead of the 1/3 unit of wheat in the original tableau.

Marx's Approach Defeated

If we insist, as Bortkiewicz (1949), Seton (1957), Morishima (1973), Medio (1972), and others who adopt the same arguments do, that the value of labor-power is the labor time actually embodied in the workers' consumption, then we must proceed differently. It is necessary to hold, not the value of money, but the real wage constant in the transformation. The equations become

$$p_s = [1+r]([1/2]p_s + w) \tag{6.8}$$

$$p_w = [1+r]([1/4]p_s + w) \tag{6.9}$$

$$w = [1/3]p_w \tag{6.10}$$

The first two equations again require that the rate of profit be uniform, given the money wage w. The third equation now requires that the money wage be just large enough to buy 1/3 unit of wheat. It is possible to solve these equations for the profit rate r and the ratio of the prices p_s/p_w: $r = 39.45\%$ and $p_s/p_w = 1.5354$. It is now possible to choose any way of normalizing the prices. For example, we could require that the value added remain at $20,000, to make the situation comparable to the solution in the last section. In this case we find that $p_w = \$1.4452$ and $p_s = \$2.219$. The wage would be $[1/3]p_w = \$.4817$, and the final tableau would look like this:

Sector	c	v	s	c+v+s	p	s/v	r(%)
Wheat	5,547	4,817	4,088	14,452	$1.445	1 (0.85)	39.45
Steel	11,095	4,817	6,278	22,190	$2.219	1 (1.31)	39.45
Total	16,642	9,634	10,366	36,642		1.076	39.45

The profit rate has indeed been equalized, and the value of money remains the same; but the surplus value has changed from 10,000 to 10,366, corresponding to a change in the social rate of surplus value from 1 to 1.076.

It is possible to use this method to equalize profit rates for any number of commodities and any structure of input–output coefficients, but in general it is impossible to view the result as a redistribution of the original surplus value. Thus in this case even two parts of Marx's first claim, that surplus value and the rate of surplus value are conserved in the transformation, do not hold. We could, of course, have chosen the price of wheat and steel in the same ratio, but in such a way that the total surplus value was 10,000; in that case, however, the value added would have changed and the rate of surplus value would still be 1.076—different from the original 1.0.

Significance of the Transformation Problem

It may seem unlikely, but in fact the differences illustrated above have been since the publication of Volume 3 of *Capital* the main focus of technical economic discussions over the consistency of the labor theory of value and its usefulness as a framework for economic analysis. Three positions in this discussion can be identified.

First, a number of critics of the labor theory of value have insisted that the only consistent way to resolve the transformation problem is to hold the real wage constant, which is their interpretation of the passage in *Capital* (1867, pp. 170–171) concerning the determination of the value of labor-power. As we have seen, this method makes it impossible to view the transformed profit as a redistributed surplus value. The critics, notably Samuelson (1971) and Robinson (1960), take this as conclusive proof of the irrelevance of the labor theory of value to positive economic analysis. In their view the discussion of value as such adds nothing to economic analysis, which might just as well start with prices of production directly. This view ignores the notion that the labor theory of value is the idea that the total value added in a commodity-producing society is an expression of the total social labor time expended. It confuses the labor theory of value with the hypothesis of equal exchange.

Second, some defenders of the labor theory of value have accepted the solution that holds constant the real wage and hence have admitted that actual prices, insofar as they are governed by the equalization of rates of profit, have only a distant and distorted relation to true labor values. These defenders insist, however, that there is a qualitative relation between the labor value accounting scheme and real prices, in the sense that real profit rates will be positive if and only if surplus value calculated in labor values is also positive—Morishima (1973) calls this relation the Fundamental Marxian Theorem. The adherents of this view accept, as a result, a much-weakened empirical role for the labor theory of value.

Finally, proponents of the position that the value of labor-power is the money wage multiplied by the value of money—for example, Dumenil (1980), Lipietz (1982), and Foley (1982)—argue that the essential point in Marx's treatment is the idea that the value added exactly represents the total social labor time and that the surplus value exactly corresponds to unpaid labor time. Because they use the first method of completing Marx's approach, which exhibits these invariances, these economists argue that there is nothing to prevent one from using the labor theory of value as a consistent and exact theoretical framework for empirical economic analysis. In fact, from this point of view the equalization of the rate of profit is irrelevant. Whatever market prices happen to be, even if competition among capitals fails in important ways, the labor theory of value is an accurate and powerful account of the aggregate relations of capitalist production. The issues raised by the deviation of prices from labor values are secondary problems of the distribution of the surplus value through unequal exchange.

Summary

The profit rate is the form in which surplus value and its determinants appear to the participants in the capitalist economic system. In this form the connection between surplus value and unpaid labor time is obscured. Capital itself appears to be the source and regulator of the amount of profit: those who own a lot of capital get a proportionately large share of the surplus value.

But what is invisible at the level of the individual worker or individual capitalist firm becomes apparent when we move to a social viewpoint. Then the connection between the total social surplus value and the division of social labor time between workers and capitalists is understandable. This connection suggests powerful determinants for the rate of profit and its movements, linking the rate of profit to the productivity of labor and the standard of living of workers through the concept of the value of labor-power.

The orthodox economic critique of the labor theory of value rests on the assertion that it is impossible logically to maintain the connection between surplus value and unpaid labor time in general models of production. We have seen that this critique rests in turn on two basic ideas. First is the illegitimate conflation of the labor theory of value (the claim that the social value added represents the social labor time) with the hypothesis of equal exchange (the notion that the money prices of all commodities accurately reflect their labor values). Second is the insistence that the value of labor-power be interpreted as the concrete labor embodied in the commodities workers consume rather than as the amount of abstract social labor workers receive in wages in exchange for 1 hour of labor-power. We have seen that it is possible logically to interpret the value of labor-power in the second way and under that assumption to demonstrate rigorously the quantitative connection between surplus value and unpaid labor time.

There seems no reason specific to the transformation problem for abandoning the labor theory of value as a practical, operational framework for the explanatory analysis of capitalist economic relations.

7

The Division of Surplus Value

The Forms of Surplus Value
(Capital 3.16–3.18, 3.21–3.25, 3.37–3.45)

In real capitalist societies we observe many important streams of revenue that appear to have nothing to do with the direct exploitation of workers. The owner of unimproved land collects a rent, even if not a single hour of labor has ever been expended on his property. The owner of money can lend it out at interest, never entering the labor market as a capitalist or organizing any production whatsoever. Many firms earn substantial commercial profits merely from the shrewd buying and selling of already produced commodities, even if during the period of their ownership of the commodity it is completely untouched by labor. These revenues play a central role in capitalist society. They form the niches in which many people find their actual means of social existence. Thus we must understand their exact relation to capitalist production if we want to grasp the inner workings of a capitalist economy.

Each of the cases mentioned in the preceding paragraph poses a challenge to the labor theory of value because in each case the revenue is separated from the actual exploitation of workers in production. Marx thus wants to analyze them to show the adequacy of the labor theory of value and the theory of surplus value to explain the whole range of economic phenomena in capitalist society. In each case Marx's explanation takes the same form. He argues that these revenues arise because the agents who collect them are in a position to bargain some of the surplus value created in production away from the industrial capitalists who initially appropriate it. All these forms of revenue—rent, interest, and commercial profit—are viewed in Marx's framework as deductions from a surplus value already given in magnitude by the value of labor-power and the amount of social labor time expended. The theoretical problem in these cases is to show how the particular form of revenue arises and to explain its behavior.

Rent   *(Capital 3.37–3.45)*

Differential Rent and Equalization of Profit Rates   *(Capital 3.38)*

Marx's concept of the price of production shows how profit rates in a capitalist system of production can be equalized when all the capitalists have access to the same techniques of production. In real capitalist societies different capitals have access to different techniques. First of all, there are always some capitalist producers who are ahead of the average in their adoption of new techniques of production. This problem Marx discusses at some length in his analysis of the dynamic tendency for the rate of profit to fall, as we shall see in Chapter 8. But capitalist producers may also differ in their access to techniques because of natural differences in the productivity of particular resources. In agriculture, for example, land varies in fertility. In mining, access to rich ores lowers the labor inputs required to yield a given output. If all capitalist producers face the same prices for labor-power and other inputs to production and the same prices for their products, those who have access to superior resources will have lower costs and hence higher profit rates. How is this compatible with the tendency for competition among capitalists to equalize profit rates?

Marx begins his analysis of this problem by supposing (anachronistically) that there is initially no property right in the superior resources. Anyone can herd their cattle on the best grazing land, or drive a mineshaft into the rich seam of mineral ore, or run an oil well into an oil pool. Under these conditions the superior resources will be congested and overused; but all capitals will have access to the same technology and the profit rate will be equalized. Modern resource allocation theory views this situation as the "tragedy of the commons," and emphasizes the inefficiency in the allocation of resources that results when congestion takes place. Marx, on the other hand, sees this situation as the ground on which a new social relation, between the resource owner and the capitalist, will emerge.

Suppose now that a property right in the scarce superior resources is established. This means that a particular person or agent is given the right to exclude producers from access to the superior resource. The resource owner can bargain for a share of the surplus value that the capitalist producer can appropriate by using the superior resource. In fact, the resource owner can always secure in this bargain the whole of the extra surplus value available as a result of the reduction in cost made possible by the use of his resource. As long as the rent is lower than this, the capitalist has an incentive to use the resource; if it is higher, the capitalist will go elsewhere.

Marx illustrates this theory by analyzing the situation of the owner of a waterfall that can be used as the power source for a mill. Suppose that the alternative method of production is to power the mill by a steam engine and that the cost of a unit of output with the steam technology is $90. If the rate of profit is 33.33% and the rate of turnover of capital is 1 (that is, the cost is also the capital invested), the price of the output (as long as the steam technology is actually in use) will be $120, that is, equal to the cost of $90 plus the profit of $30 (33.33% of $90). If a capitalist uses the waterfall, he avoids some of the costs he must pay to use steam. Suppose that the cost of production using the waterfall is only $60. In the absence of rent, the waterfall producer will appropriate a profit of $60 on each unit of output. The waterfall producer's rate of profit would be 100%, well above the average rate of profit of 33.33%. Thus, Marx argues, the waterfall owner will be in a position to bargain for a rent of $40 per unit of output, leaving the capitalist $20 profit on his cost of $60 for production with the waterfall— exactly the same as with steam—and equalizing the waterfall rate of profit to the average.

The important conclusion generated by this analysis is that rent is a socially created revenue and does not correspond to any power of the land to produce value. If, for example, the cost of production with steam declined to $60 in the situation just analyzed, the ability of the waterfall owner to appropriate a rent would disappear, even

though the waterfall retained exactly the same productive properties. If there were no property right in the waterfall, its potential
productivity would remain the same, but there would be no rent.

This analysis of differential rent is similar in its basic outline to
Ricardo's theory of rent, although Marx had significant reserva-
tions about some of the conclusions Ricardo tried to draw from the
theory.

Absolute Rent (Capital 3.45)

Marx also spends some time analyzing the issue of absolute rent,
a concept that is somewhat mysterious from the point of view of
modern social relations. An absolute rent is a money charge for
access to a resource exacted by a landowner independent of its
relative productivity. This kind of charge played an important role
in the politics of rural social relations in Germany in the nineteenth century; hence Marx was concerned with it, although it
plays a very minor role, at least in advanced capitalist countries in
the twentieth century.

Landowners can enforce absolute rents only if they collude,
either through private agreement or through legal restraints. In
the absence of collusion competition among landowners will force
the absolute component of rent to zero. Marx expresses this point
by saying that absolute rent is a class phenomenon and reflects the
power relations of landowners organized as a class in relation to
peasants and capitalist farmers. Only as a class can the landowners enforce an access fee that is independent of the actual productivity of the land.

Rent as Social Surplus Value (Capital 3.37)

Insofar as rent is paid by capitalists (whether it is differential rent
or absolute rent) it is a part of the social surplus value. Its existence
does not alter the general principles governing the production of
value or the appropriation of surplus value that Marx has already
developed.

It is true that the existence of rent on scarce resources will have
an effect on the price of production as compared with a situation
in which there are no property rights in scarce superior resources
and in which all capitalists have access to the same techniques. As

the waterfall example shows, the individual capitalist counts rent as a deduction from gross profit. The price of production will have to rise to the point at which capital can appropriate the average rate of profit on the least good resources in use; and the rents on better resources will adjust accordingly to level the rate of profit on capitals employed with them.

In the absence of scarce appropriated resources that yield rents, it is possible to calculate the prices of production for a capitalist system without knowing anything about the pattern of allocation of social capital across sectors. This calculation is possible because cost conditions will not change as capital is moved from one sector to another. But with scarce appropriated resources the scale of production in a sector will influence the quality of the marginal resource used and hence the price of production in that sector. If in the waterfall example the social output of the mill sector declined to the point at which no steam producers were in operation and the waterfall was the highest cost production method in use, the price of the output would fall until the waterfall producer earned the average rate of profit on its lower costs and capital invested. The rent would disappear and the price of production in that sector would change.

Interest   *(Capital 3.21–3.25)*

Interest and Lending   *(Capital 3.21–3.22)*

When one economic agent lends money to another, the lender is often in a position to bargain for the repayment, not just of the sum lent, but of additional money called *interest*. Interest is the simplest form of surplus value because nothing mediates between the advance of money and the appropriation of the interest. In Marx's diagrammatic terms, the form of interest is

$$M - M + \Delta M \tag{7.1}$$

where M is the money lent, or the principal, and ΔM is the interest, or surplus value repaid along with the principal. When we divide the interest by the principal and by the time period for which the loan runs, we get a pure rate of return, the *interest rate*. If, for example, the lender lends \$1000 for 1 year and receives

$1100 at the end of the year, the interest is $100 and the interest rate 10% per year.

The form of interest is probably as old as money and hence as old as the commodity form itself. But in different societies the motives of borrowers and lenders may differ, and the principles that explain the interest rate may differ as well. For example, in ancient Rome the borrower was often an heir who wanted to spend some of the estate eventually due before the death of its owner. The interest payment on the loan in this case presumably included an insurance premium element to protect the lender against the possibility that the heir would die first. In traditional agricultural societies peasants who face a poor harvest often borrow to ensure their physical survival. In modern capitalist society the great bulk of lending and borrowing is done by capitalist firms, whose motive is the appropriation of surplus value and economic survival when threatened by bankruptcy. But important amounts of lending and borrowing involve households, which borrow to finance house ownership and consumption, and the State.

Because the payment of interest involves the transfer of value for which there is no commodity equivalent, interest must always have its basis in unequal exchange or in exploitation. The exploitation may be direct or indirect. The poor peasant borrower, who pays interest out of his own labor and its product, is exploited directly. The Roman heir, who pays the interest eventually out of the revenues of the estate (which are based on the exploitation of slaves) and the capitalist firm, which pays interest out of the surplus value it appropriates from wage labor, pay interest by exploiting someone else. The analysis of interest as based in exploitation or in unequal exchange says nothing about the motives that prompt the borrowing transaction: both parties to that transaction may be very satisfied with it and may feel that the opportunity to borrow and lend is an entirely good thing. But from a social point of view the value transferred has to arise from social labor, and the form of interest shows that there is no direct equivalent labor time given up by the agent who receives the interest.

Interest in Capitalist Production   *(Capital 3.23)*

Although household and State borrowing are significant in advanced capitalist society, Marx focuses his attention on borrowing by capitalist firms, taking the view that these transactions are the dominant and determining element in the formation of the rate of interest. The capitalist borrows in the first instance in order to use the money received as money capital, to commit it to the circuit of capital and to appropriate a surplus value as a result. When borrowing is involved, we can extend Marx's diagram of the circuit of capital to

$$M_0 - M - C\{LP, MP\} \ldots (P) \ldots C' - M' - M_0' \qquad (7.2)$$

M_0 represents the original money of the lender, which is transferred to the capitalist borrower, then passes like other money capital through the circuit of capital, and participates in the appropriation of surplus value. M_0' is the repayment of principal and interest by the capitalist borrower to the capitalist lender.

Thus Marx concludes that interest payments by capitalist firms are a part of the surplus value appropriated in capitalist production. Not all the interest payments made in a capitalist society, however, are interest payments by capitalist firms. Worker households, for example, may borrow in order to buy houses or finance consumption spending. They pay the interest directly from their wages. Interest in this kind of transaction surely represents exploitation, because the worker household gives up some claim to social labor time without an equivalent; but it is not exploitation through the sale and purchase of labor-power. Again, to say that the interest is rooted in exploitation is not to say that there is anything unfair or involuntary about the transaction (any more than the wage-labor bargain is formally unequal). Both the worker and the lender may be quite happy with the loan transaction, given the social situations they find themselves in. The borrowing of the State is paid back out of State revenues. To understand the source of this surplus value, we have to look at the source of the State revenues, which may be the sharing of capitalist surplus value through taxation, or taxes on wages, or surplus value arising in State-organized capitalist production.

Externalization of the Interest Rate *(Capital 3.24)*

In well-developed capitalist economies, borrowing and lending become routine and bureaucratized features of everyday business. Competition among borrowers on one side and lenders on the other forms a market rate of interest that, like any other market price, appears to be external to the decisions of all the agents involved. Although the source of interest is actually in the surplus value appropriated by individual capitalists, each capitalist sees the interest rate as a coercive fact external to himself. This process creates several of the more mystifying illusions of capitalist society.

First of all, the capitalist is led to divide his own surplus value between the part that represents the interest he could have received had he lent his own capital and the rest (which may be positive or negative). The residual Marx calls *profit of enterprise,* that is, the surplus value that is left over once interest at the market rate has been paid on the money capital invested. Because the capitalist could have lent his own money capital out at the market rate of interest, the interest component of the surplus value appears to be a return to money as such, independent of the production decisions the capitalist makes. The profit of enterprise, however, rises or falls directly with the good or bad fortune and good or bad judgment of the capitalist himself and thus appears to be a return to his own direct superintendence of the process of production. This is an important source of the idea in capitalist society that profit (that is, profit of enterprise) is a return to management, or risk-taking, or the wages of superintendence, rather than a part of the social surplus value arising from the exploitation of workers.

The capitalist does not have to borrow money in order to see the interest rate as a cost. Because he could have lent his money capital at the rate of interest, the interest rate appears to be an opportunity cost to him of using his own capital in his own production process. If he manages to achieve a rate of profit just equal to the market interest rate, in a sense he has nothing to show for his pains even though from a social point of view he has contributed to the appropriation of the social surplus value.

Once the interest rate emerges as a social fact, every agent in capitalist society is compelled to view money as potentially expanding value, which could grow at the rate of interest if it were lent. Thus the rate of interest constitutes an opportunity cost for every spending decision throughout the economy, not just for the capitalist. Everyone must constantly weigh any given proposed expenditure against the option of letting the money grow at the rate of interest. This necessity creates a systematic bias against expenditures whose benefits arrive in the future, after some time delay. Economists, observing this pervasive tendency in capitalist society to discount future benefits, call the resulting behavior *time preference*. In fact some economists have tried to argue that the rate of interest is caused by an inborn time preference in the psychological makeup of the individual human beings. Marx argues that the real situation is just the opposite: it is the emergence of an interest rate on the basis of the appropriation of surplus value that creates a time preference in the decisions of individuals in capitalist society.

Determination of the Interest Rate

In an economy dominated by capitalist production, the main borrowers and lenders are capitalist firms. Households and the State may participate in the huge market for funds created by capitalist borrowing and lending, but Marx's presumption is that the interest rate is formed in the bargaining between capitalist firms, some acting as lenders on one side, some acting as borrowers on the other. The existence of banks or other financial intermediaries does not change this picture significantly. Instead of bargaining directly with each other, the borrower and lender each bargain independently with the intermediary over the level of the interest rate.

Marx argues that there is no general scientific principle that determines the level of the interest rate in relation to the profit rate.

> The average rate of interest prevailing in a certain country—as distinct from the continually fluctuating market rates—cannot be determined by any law. In this sphere there is no such thing as a natural rate of interest in the sense in which economists speak of a natural rate of profit and a natural rate of wages . . . There is no good reason why average conditions of competition, the balance between lender and borrower, should give the lender an interest of 3, 4, 5%, etc., or else a certain percentage of the gross profits, say 20% or 50%, on his capital. Wherever it is competition as such which determines anything, the determination is accidental, purely empirical, and only pedantry or fantasy would seek to represent this accident as a necessity. (1894, pp. 362–363)

Under usual conditions the interest could not exceed the whole surplus value appropriated, because borrowers would then have no incentive to borrow. Similarly, the interest rate could not fall below zero, because lenders would then have no incentive to lend.

At the risk of venturing into the realm of pedantry and fantasy, we might seek to extend Marx's account of the rate of interest in certain directions. First, under twentieth-century conditions, the interest rate in value terms might fall below zero, because many potential lenders have no secure way to hold value at a zero rate of return. The potential lender in a modern monetary system must either lend to a bank or to the State by holding currency or transform its wealth into a stock of physical commodities, which are costly to maintain, protect, and liquidate. Marx is clearly thinking of a commodity money system, where a lender can choose to hold gold at a low cost, instead of lending.

Second, there may be some important systematic principles governing the level of the interest rate, given the rate of profit. If capitalist firms faced no uncertainties in the production and realization of value, they would presumably bid the interest rate to equality with the average rate of profit, allowing for whatever costs might be incurred in actually making a loan. A capitalist firm that was sure of appropriating the average rate of profit on a loan would have an incentive to borrow as long as the interest rate was below that profit rate and would have no incentive to lend until the interest rate reached the average rate of profit.

But in reality the appropriation of surplus value at the level of the individual capital is far from certain, and the capital faces the prospect of economic annihilation through bankruptcy if it is chronically unable to realize enough surplus value to cover its interest obligations. Under these conditions the rate of interest may differ from the rate of profit, depending on the distribution of capitalist firms with respect to the risk of bankruptcy and their realized profit rates.

Marx's theory of the interest rate is in the tradition of loanable funds theories, which emphasize the formation of the rate of interest in transactions in new loans at any moment in time; it contrasts with liquidity preference theories (Keynes, 1936), which argue that the interest rate is formed primarily in secondary markets for old loans.

Fictitious Capital

Once an interest rate has emerged from the welter of borrowing and lending transactions, it produces further curious economic effects. Any stream of revenue, whether or not it arises from the appropriation of surplus value in capitalist production, will command a price—its *capitalized value*—that depends on the interest rate.

Take for example a State bond. The State creates an income stream by promising to pay $100 a year to the holder of its bond. If the interest rate is 10% and the stream is expected to continue indefinitely (as in the case of a "consol"—a bond without maturity), an investor will be willing to pay $1,000 for the bond. This $1,000 looks like a capital to the investor because he pays it out in return for the stream of interest payments from the State; but it corresponds to no value actually invested in capitalist production because the interest is being paid out of the revenues of the State. Marx refers to this capitalized value as a *fictitious capital* because it appears to its owner to be a capital value but in fact represents no real part of the social productive capital.

Several similar phenomena have considerable importance. The common stock of a publicly held corporation gives its owners the right to a share of the dividend payments made by the corporation. The relation between these dividend payments and the actual profit of enterprise of the corporation is not very close, because the management can decide to pay out a large or a small part of the profit of enterprise as dividends or to pay a more stable stream of dividends than the stream of profit of enterprise. The market will capitalize the prospective stream of dividends at the going rate of interest, just as it capitalizes the interest paid on the State debt. The resulting capital value may greatly exceed the value of the capital actually invested by the corporation, the excess being a fictitious capital. The vicissitudes of fictitious capital provide some of the most dramatic episodes in finance. If the interest rate rises, for example, tremendous amounts of fictitious capital may simply disappear, despite the fact that the capital actually invested in production may have changed not at all or only a little.

The price of land including all productive natural resources is a similar case. Because the ownership of scarce productive resources allows the appropriation of a stream of rental income, the market will also capitalize this stream in relation to the interest rate. In this way substantial wealth in private terms is created without any social counterpart in accumulated capital.

Commercial Profit: Productive and Unproductive Labor
(Capital 3.16–3.19)

Profit without Production   *(Capital 3.16)*

The third major case in which agents appropriate a revenue without directly exploiting workers involves *commercial capital*. The commercial capitalist profits by buying and selling existing commodities without transforming them productively in any way. For example commodity brokers may profit from buying, say, vegetable oil stored in tanks, holding it for a time, and then selling it, without anything having happened to the vegetable oil as a result.

This *commercial profit* is a puzzle for the labor theory of value because no labor has been expended to create new value. Thus the question arises as to where the surplus value that is appropriated by the commercial capital as a profit comes from.

This problem does not arise in the case in which the capital is involved in transportation or communication services. Moving a commodity from one point to another does alter its use-value and is an aspect of production. Communication services that are essential to production processes are, like raw materials, a direct input into production. In many cases the same capital is involved both in making a profit by transporting and transforming the commodity (say, distributing it in smaller units), which are productive activities, and in making a profit purely from buying and selling the commodity, which are not productive activities. In these cases the problem of commercial profit is restricted to that part of the capital's profit that corresponds to the pure buying and selling activity.

Origin of Commercial Profit in Unequal Exchange   *(Capital 3.17)*

Marx explains commercial profit within the framework of the labor theory of value as arising from unequal exchange. He argues that the commercial capital buys commodities below their values (or prices of production) and sells them at their value. The difference is the source of revenue for the commercial capital.

As is usually the case with unequal exchange, this situation need not be viewed as detrimental to the interests of the commodity producers who sell the commodities below their values. A producing capitalist could internalize the functions of commercial capital and sell the commodities it produces to their final consumers. But there are a variety of reasons why this may be costly or inconvenient. The producer may command considerable knowledge and skills concerning the production process, its technology, the mobilization of a productive labor force, and so on without knowing very much about markets and distribution. Thus it may be cheaper to sell the commodity to a middleman somewhat below its full value than to hold on to it until the final consumer buys it.

From this point of view the emergence of commercial capital as a separate sector of capital amounts to the splitting off of one of the nodes of the circuit of capital diagram. In a similar way, the emergence of financial capital as a separate category corresponds to the splitting off of the money capital node in the circuit of capital. Historically we see oscillations in the degree of independence from productive capital achieved by these two nodes. At times commercial capital and financial capital may be powerful and well developed in relation to small and disorganized productive capitals. At other times the consolidation of productive capital may lead it to try to reabsorb the financial and commercial functions.

The important analytical consequence of this view of the profit of commercial capital is the claim that the determinants of profitability of commercial capital are different from the determinants of profitability of productive capital. If we analyze the profitability of productive capital we will be led to consider changes in the productivity of labor, the organization of the production process, and the level of wages. If we analyze the profitability of commercial capital, we will find that it turns on the special knowledge or competitive position the commercial capital has in relation to the market.

Commercial Capital and Profit Rate Equalization   (*Capital 3.17*)

Despite the fact that the underlying determinants of the profitability of commercial capital are different from those of productive capital, commercial capital still participates in the equalization of the rate of profit. To make a profit by buying and selling commodities, a commercial capitalist must tie up a certain amount of capital; and that capital will tend to command the average rate of profit. To the degree that a separate sector of commercial capital develops, competition among the commercial capitals will tend to narrow the degree of unequal exchange until the revenues of commercial capitals just suffice to cover the average rate of profit.

This effect strengthens the illusion that capital itself, rather than labor, produces value. In extreme cases it is dramatically obvious that the profit of commercial capital has nothing whatever to do with the expenditure of labor or of production. Marx's explanation shows how the profit on commercial capital can be seen as part of the surplus value that is created and appropriated by productive capital but is shared, as it were, with the commercial capital.

Productive and Unproductive Labor (Capital 1.16, 3.17)

Commercial activities, once they have reached a certain scale, require labor as well as capital. The execution of buying and selling transactions, record-keeping, and acquisition of market information all require human time and effort. But from a social point of view these activities do not add to the total output of use-values; they are concerned with the struggle to redistribute value and surplus value once it has been produced.

Marx takes up a distinction emphasized by Adam Smith—that between *productive* and *unproductive labor*. Smith (1776, bk. 2, chap. 3), however, gave several partial definitions of productive labor that are not consistent with one another. His starting point is the contrast between the labor hired by a capitalist and the labor provided by domestic servants. The industrial worker produces a commodity, which will be sold on the market to recover its costs of production and reap a surplus value, whereas the domestic servant performs direct services for his employer but produces nothing for the market. Smith called the first kind of labor *productive*, in the sense that it repaid its own costs and yielded a surplus value, and the second kind *unproductive*, in the sense that it consumed value rather than adding to it. Smith unfortunately confounded this relatively clear distinction by raising another, quite different one—that between labor producing a physical product and labor producing a service. The trouble is that labor that produces a service that is sold on the market for a price that exceeds its costs is just as productive in the first sense as labor that produces a durable physical object for sale. Finally, Smith made an important distinction between the private and social points of view, arguing that productive labor increased social wealth, whereas unproductive labor consumed it. In this context he makes his famous remark that the King of England, like the army, navy, and State bureaucracy in general, is an unproductive laborer, because he consumes rather than produces social wealth. The trouble here is that labor may be employed to yield a surplus value to a particular capitalist, even though from a social point of view it is unproductive. For example, labor engaged in commodity advertising may be completely socially unproductive if the advertising efforts of two competitors have equivalent but opposite effects, thereby canceling each other. But if advertising services are produced as a commodity by firms organized for that purpose, the labor expended on them does return its own costs and a surplus value to the capitalist who employs it—although this surplus value is actually transferred from productive sectors.

Marx takes Smith's confusion as the occasion to make a kind of dialectical joke. First, he says, every mode of production will define productive and unproductive labor in its own way and in conformity to its own logic. The trouble, he argues, is that Smith does not recognize that he is describing a specifically capitalist economy, in which the notion of productivity is firmly attached to value or surplus value productivity. Whereas in a more rationally organized society the word *productive* might have something to do with activities that meet human needs, in capitalist society it gets attached to activities that produce a surplus value. Marx argues that to reconstruct this distinction rationally we must view as productive in capitalist society that labor which adds to the social surplus value and hence to the potential accumulation of capital.

This position, to begin with, rejects the distinction between production of durable objects and services that confuses Smith's account. Services, like transportation or communication, may contribute just as much to social surplus value as production of durable physical objects. But it goes beyond Smith's first definition by insisting on a social test for the production of surplus value. The advertising labor described above certainly produces a surplus value for its particular capitalist, but equally clearly it consumes rather than adds to the social surplus value; and thus it should be viewed as unproductive.

It is extremely important to remember that Marx, in reconstructing Smith's distinction, is not endorsing it as a universal category. In another mode of production a different set of categories would presumably evolve to define social productivity. But the definition of productive labor as labor that produces a surplus value from the social point of view makes sense within capitalist production and is important in the analysis of capital accumulation.

It is also important to recognize that having an adequate and consistent definition of productive labor does not solve the problem of actually measuring it in concrete situations. Many cases may be relatively uncontroversial, but there will always be borderline cases that are not at all easy to resolve. Everyone, especially in twentieth-century capitalist societies, might concede that liveried servants represent a consumption of social product and hence ought to be viewed as unproductive labor. But what about scientists and engineers working in basic research? Their product, fundamental knowledge, does not take the form of a commodity and is not directly sold on the market. The resources they use in the form of their own wages, those of laboratory assistants and equipment and space are formally paid out of surplus value in most modern corporations. Thus a case could be made for viewing basic research as unproductive in the strict sense of the term.

Useful, Necessary, and Productive Labor

The last example indicates how careful we have to be about the meaning of theoretical terms in this area. Many people react to it by arguing that because basic research is vital to modern capitalist society and is a necessary precondition for increases in productivity and standards of living, it is absurd to classify it as unproductive. Adam Smith's readers had less trouble with his assertion that the King of England was unproductive.

To try to unravel this tangle, both Marx and Smith make a distinction between *useful, necessary,* and *productive* labor. Take the State bureaucracy (including the King), for example. Smith argues that these functionaries may be quite necessary to keep the society going even though they are unproductive. In the same way Marx argues that military forces may be quite necessary to the reproduction of capitalist society, even though they consume rather than produce surplus value.

There are also many laboring activities that are extremely useful but must be viewed as unproductive in capitalist society because they do not produce a commodity that is sold on the market. The labor of childcare and housekeeping, for example, is obviously necessary for the reproduction of the society and is extremely useful. But because this labor is most often performed within family relations of production, it usually does not result in a saleable product or produce a surplus value directly; hence it is unproductive. Like the research scientist or the advertising copywriter, the housekeeper can be viewed as contributing indirectly to the production of surplus value (say, by keeping the costs of reproduction of labor-power low). But if we extend the meaning of productive labor to every activity that contributes in any indirect way to the reproduction of capital, there would be hardly any unproductive activities at all. It seems better either to stick to a narrow but meaningful definition of productive labor or to abandon the distinction altogether.

This distinction will not make any sense if one takes the position that any activity that secures a revenue must correspond to the production of a good or service, as, for example, most neoclassical economists hold. This position is, in fact, of a piece with the neoclassical view that land and capital produce a certain part of the value added because the owners of land and capital are in a position to appropriate some part of that value. In the same way, these economists argue that producers of financial services or of advertising, because they command a price in the market, produce a good or service in the same sense as producers of food or clothing do. The one exception to this view for neoclassical economists is the State bureaucracy, whose revenues they view as arising from compulsion through the tax system and hence as not productive of value.

The Exploitation of Unproductive Workers (Capital 3.17)

Despite the fact that wage-laborers in such sectors as trade, financial services, and advertising cannot be viewed as adding to the social surplus value (or value added) and as a result are unproductive, these same workers (we shall call them unproductive workers, for convenience) are exploited in the same way as productive workers. Exploitation through the wage labor relation occurs when a worker expends more labor hours than he or she receives an equivalent for in wages. The unproductive worker is in this respect exactly like the productive worker. If an unproductive worker expends 2,000 hours in a year and if the value of money is 1/15 hour per dollar, the money equivalent of that labor time is $30,000. If the worker's wage is, say, $15,000 a year, which represents 1,000 hours of social labor time, one-half the labor time he or she expends is unpaid, just like that of a productive worker.

It may be very difficult for a worker to perceive the degree of social productiveness of a job. A clerk who moves from filing production scheduling records (productive labor, because production scheduling is part of the direct production process) to filing tax forms (unproductive labor, because the processing of tax forms concerns the distribution rather than the creation of new value) probably experiences little change of consciousness. The critical point is that both the productive and unproductive worker under capitalist relations of production give up their whole labor time to their employer and receive wages that are an equivalent for only part of that labor time.

Value Flows in the U.S. Economy, 1983

We can use the ideas presented in this chapter to get some sense of value production and value flows in an advanced capitalist economy. The numbers I shall use roughly reflect the situation of the economy of the United States in 1983 as reported in the *Economic Report of the President* (1984), but they are rounded and altered to give a suggestive rather than a precise picture.

The population of the United States in 1983 was about 235 million people, of whom about 175 million were over 16 years of age and not institutionalized. Of this potential work force, about 100 million people had jobs and about 10 million were unemployed and actively looking for jobs. Thus we could say that the latent reserve army was about 65 million people and the floating reserve army about 10 million in the United States in 1983.

Of the 100 million employed, about half were engaged in productive labor and about half in unproductive labor. (Wolff, 1986, chap. 5, estimates that in 1976 over half of total employment was either in unproductive sectors or in unproductive jobs in productive sectors.) The 50 million productively employed people worked about 83 billion hours in the whole year.

In this time they produced about $2,500 billion in new value (not counting the wages of government workers as part of value added). The total value produced per person of the population exceeded $10,000. Thus each productive worker produced about $50,000 of new value in a year, or about $30 worth of value added in each hour of work. (This implies that the value of money was about 1/30, or 2 minutes of productive labor contained in each dollar of value added.) The wages of these productive workers amounted to about $1,000 billion, about $20,000 per productive worker per year, or about $12 per hour. These numbers include fringe benefits of various kinds, so that actual take-home pay was somewhat smaller. These productive workers, whose wages were $1,000 billion, produced about $1,500 billion in surplus value. Thus the average rate of exploitation of productive workers was approximately 1.5 (150%). Productive workers worked 1.5 hours producing surplus value for each hour they worked to produce the equivalent of their wages.

What happened to this enormous mass of surplus value? The largest share, $1,000 billion, went to pay the wages of unproductive workers in business and government. Rental and proprietors' incomes took about $100 billion, net interest amounted to about $250 billion, and profit of enterprise, after all taxes, was about $150 billion. These numbers reflect some surprising paradoxes of economic development. The United States economy has reached very high absolute levels of labor productivity, and as a result the rate of surplus value and the mass of surplus value are both extremely large. But most of this surplus value is consumed in the process of distributing the product and coping with the conflicts engendered in the production of the value. As a result, a relatively small amount of value finally takes the form of property income, and an even smaller amount can be directly disposed of by capitalists in the form of profit of enterprise.

These numbers also emphasize how much difference it makes whether one systematically accounts for the phenomenon of unproductive labor in observing a capitalist economy. If we viewed all employed labor as productive, we would have a surplus value of only $500 billion, and the rate of exploitation would be only 0.25 (25%). From Marx's point of view, this way of looking at things gravely underestimates both the productivity reached by the capitalist system and the surplus value it can achieve.

8

The Falling Rate of Profit

The Character of Capitalist Production   *(Capital 3.13)*

Marx was interested in the ways in which human societies change as they develop. For him, to understand a social process was, above all, to understand its characteristic pattern of movement. The labor theory of value, including the specific cases of simple and expanded reproduction, provides an accounting framework that can be used to describe what happens in capitalist production but that does not address directly the question of qualitative change.

Marx had a distinctive and well-formulated view of the essential character of capitalist production, that is, he saw capitalism as a *technically progressive* mode of production. This idea appears vividly in the *Communist Manifesto* (Marx and Engels, 1848) and throughout all of Marx's writings about capitalist society. Earlier class societies never institutionalized technical change to the degree that capitalism does. Capitalist society accepts the constant revolutionizing of its methods of production and with it the constant rise and fall of the fortunes of particular capitalists, as the central energy that keeps the system as a whole going. Marx saw capitalist society as having the historical mission of developing forces of production, including technology.

Thus a full understanding of capitalist production requires not only the analysis of the source of surplus value in the exploitation of workers and the construction of the circuit of capital as the mode of reproduction of capital but also a knowledge of the effects of technical progress on social relations and circulation. In quantitative terms technical change alters the parameters that govern exploitation and the circuit of capital, the rate of surplus value, the composition of capital outlays, the rate of capitalization of surplus value, and the turnover times of the various phases of the circuit of capital.

The Consequences of Capital Accumulation   (Capital 3.13)

Marx gives a rapid sketch of the consequences of the establishment of capitalist social relations and the accumulation of capital in *Capital* (1894, chap. 13). To begin with, he argues, capitalists simply take over relatively unproductive technical methods of production that they inherit from previous modes of production. These methods are incapable of providing very large surplus labor times precisely because labor is deployed so ineffectively in them. But they also have the advantage, for the capitalist, of requiring very small capital outlays for anything except labor. Thus we would expect this first stage of capitalist production to exhibit relatively low rates of exploitation and at the same time a relatively large wage share in capital outlays, or a high composition of capital outlays. Despite the low rates of exploitation, the markup on capital advances may be high because the markup q is the product of the rate of exploitation and the composition of capital outlays: $q = ek$. The rate of profit, if rates of turnover are not too slow, may be quite high.

Capital accumulation proceeds, systematically altering methods of production (we shall look at Marx's account of this process in more detail in a moment). Marx argues that the net effect, after a considerable period of time, will be the transformation of methods of production that have much higher labor productivity and that use much larger quantities and somewhat larger values, of nonlabor inputs. The dramatic increase in the productivity of labor permits much larger surplus labor times and hence much higher rates of surplus value. This is true, although Marx does not emphasize it, even if the real standard of living of workers rises in the process. These new methods of production will require much more nonlabor input for each unit of labor input; consequently the proportion of capital outlays represented by wages will fall. Marx thought that at the end of a long period of accumulation the profile of parameters of the circuit of capital would change and the rate of exploitation e would be a good deal higher, the composition of capital outlays k much lower, and the markup, $q = ek$, also lower.

The important point is Marx's insistence that this pattern of change in production is not accidental, or random, but a systematic effect of capital accumulation itself, through its technical progressivity. He argued that the characteristic pattern of development of capitalist society involved rising labor productivity, real wages that rose more slowly than labor productivity and hence a rising rate of surplus value, a falling proportion of capital outlays devoted to wages, and a lower markup and rate of profit. Almost everyone recognizes the relevance of this pattern to the actual development of capitalist society, but great controversy has arisen over the last point—the claim that the rate of profit has a tendency to fall over time.

Marx thought of this whole collection of changes as aspects of a single inner tendency in capitalist development. Because Smith and especially Ricardo had put great emphasis on the falling rate of profit, Marx referred to this whole pattern as the tendency for the rate of profit to fall. Marx did not discover this tendency himself, but took it over as a stylized fact already well-established in the work of the political economists. When he refers to the law of the falling rate of profit as the most important discovery of modern political economy, he is asserting its importance first of all in the work of Ricardo and Smith.

Ricardo's Theory of the Falling Rate of Profit

Marx couches his discussion of the falling rate of profit as a critique of Ricardo's theory. Hence it will be easier to understand the main points Marx makes if we review Ricardo's argument.

Ricardo (1817) begins by considering an economy in which there is only one product, corn (that is, grain). A capitalist farmer advances the wages of workers in kind, by providing them with food to eat during the period that they are producing a new harvest of corn. This is the only capital outlay Ricardo explicitly considers in his basic model. The size of the corn wage is regulated by the growth of the labor force, in Malthusian fashion. There is a certain level of wages per worker that allows the workers to maintain themselves and reproduce a constant population. When the wage rises above this level, the population expands; and when it falls below, the population contracts.

The rate of profit in Ricardo is determined by the ratio of the surplus corn produced by a worker on the least productive land in use to the subsistence wage, because the wage is the only capital outlay. In Marx's terms, Ricardo is assuming that the rate of turnover of capital is 1 and that the composition of capital outlays is also 1, because wages are the only capital outlay. Under these assumptions the rate of profit is just equal to the rate of surplus value, which is the ratio of the corn surplus to the corn wage on land that has zero rent.

Once this rate of profit is established in Ricardo's model, it determines the rent on more productive land. Whatever a worker can produce on more productive land that exceeds his own wage plus the profit on that wage established by the profit rate will become a rent of the landowner. Furthermore this same profit rate becomes the average profit rate for other sectors of the system— say, manufacture—because a capitalist presumably always has the option of shifting capital into agricultural production on the marginal land.

The labor value of corn in Ricardo's model is equal to the labor time required to produce a unit of corn on the least productive land in use—the inverse of the labor productivity on that land. If less productive land were to come into use, the labor value of corn would rise. Because the equilibrium wage is a constant amount of corn, the value of labor-power would rise as well because the corn wage would represent a larger amount of labor value.

It is on this mechanism that Ricardo rests his explanation of the fall in the rate of profit with capital accumulation. The accumulation of capital increases the total wages that can be advanced by capitalists and thus the demand for labor. This bids up the wage temporarily and expands the population. But a larger population has a higher demand for food; hence agricultural production must expand to less productive land. This expansion raises the value of corn and the value of labor-power and lowers the rate of profit because the corn surplus (over the wage) produced by a worker on the less productive land will be smaller than that produced on more productive land. Ricardo carries this analysis to its logical end—the Stationary State, where the population has grown so much that a worker on the marginal land produces just enough to pay his own wage, leaves no surplus to be appropriated as profit, and the profit rate falls to zero. At this point, Ricardo argues, accumulation stops because the whole social surplus product takes the form of a rent that is consumed by the landowners.

Ricardo's theory attributes the falling rate of profit to diminishing returns with a constant technology. If technological change were to raise the productivity of labor on all land, it would clearly raise the profit rate and permit the accumulation process to proceed further.

Marx's Critique of Ricardo's Theory (Capital 3.13)

Marx's chief complaint about Ricardo's account was that it ignored the technically progressive character of capitalist production. For Marx, as we have seen, the essence of capitalist production was that it would always be adopting new techniques that raised the productivity of labor. The puzzle that Marx puts forward is to explain the fall in rate of profit precisely as a consequence of technical progress. The capitalist system routinely defeats the diminishing returns on which Ricardo puts the main emphasis, but still, in Marx's view, experiences a fall in the rate of profit.

Furthermore, Marx argues, the explanation of the falling rate of profit should not rest on a falling rate of surplus value, as it does in Ricardo's theory. The historical experience of capitalism exhibits a tendency for the rate of surplus value to rise with technical progress, as Marx urges in his discussion of relative surplus value.

But Ricardo's assumptions set the rate of profit equal to the rate of surplus value; hence there is no logical possibility of a rise in the rate of surplus value and a fall in the rate of profit. Marx argues that Ricardo's crucial error is his neglect of constant capital. Even if we hold the rate of turnover constant, the profit rate will be proportional, not to the rate of exploitation, but to the rate of exploitation multiplied by the composition of capital outlays (wages as a fraction of total capital outlays). Once we introduce the composition of capital outlays explicitly, it is possible to comprehend a process in which the rate of surplus value rises but the composition of capital outlays falls by a larger proportion, and thus the rate of profit declines. This process is, in fact, according to Marx, what we see in capitalist accumulation in real economies. Capitalism revolutionizes the process of production to increase labor productivity, but at the same time greatly increases the amount of nonlabor inputs used in production. The fall in the rate of profit is thus just another aspect of the basic process of transformation of production that lies at the heart of capitalist accumulation, along with the phenomenon of relative surplus value.

Marx's Theory of the Falling Rate of Profit (Capital 3.15)

Marx sets out to construct a theory of the dynamics of technical change under capitalism that will unify the rise in the rate of surplus value that results from relative surplus value and the fall in the rate of profit that results from the fall in the composition of capital outlays. The obvious problem in constructing such a theory is to explain why capitalists would adopt new techniques of production that lower the rate of profit. Here Marx argues that there is a crucial difference between the self-interest of individual capitalists and the long-term interests of the capitalist class as a whole. In fact, competition, according to Marx, forces individual capitalists to make decisions that appear advantageous to each one individually, but collectively result in a lower average rate of profit for the whole system. In *Capital* (1894, pp. 264–265) he sums this up as follows:

> No capitalist ever voluntarily introduces a new method of production, no matter how much more productive it may be, and how much it may increase the rate of surplus-value, so long as it reduces the rate of profit. Yet every such new method of production cheapens the commodities. Hence the capitalist sells them originally above their prices of production, or, perhaps, above their value . . . He can do this, because the average labour-time required socially for the production of these latter commodities is higher than the labour-time required for the new methods of production . . . But competition makes it general and subject to the general law. There follows a fall in the rate of profit—perhaps first in this sphere of production, and eventually it achieves a balance with the rest— which is, therefore, wholly independent of the will of the capitalist.

An individual capitalist who discovers a new technique of production that lowers costs is in a position to appropriate superprofits by continuing to sell his commodities at the going price, until other capitalists adopt the same technique and competition forces the price of the product to fall. These super-profits represent a transfer of surplus value from the higher-cost producers to the innovating capitalist. The discovery of the new technique actually lowers the social value of the commodity—by reducing the labor time socially necessary to produce it; but the backwardness of the old-fashioned producers holds the market price above the value. As a result the innovating capitalist benefits from an unequal exchange (because the price of the commodity he produces is above its value), and this high price permits him to realize surplus value that is actually produced elsewhere in the system. (We could just as easily use the words *price of production* for *social value* in the preceding argument.)

Marx argues that each capitalist is in fact forced to innovate because the capitalists are in a prisoner's dilemma situation with regard to each other. Any capitalist who forgoes a cost-reducing technical change will find himself at a competitive disadvantage if and when his competitors make a new discovery. The pressure of competition makes it certain that capitalists will pursue and adopt cost-cutting innovations. But, Marx says, the last stage of innovation is for all the competitors to adopt the new technique, thus forcing the price of the product down and eliminating the innovator's super-profit. Once this stage is complete, according to Marx, the rate of profit for the system as a whole may indeed be lower because the new technique involves more expensive nonlabor inputs. In this way it is possible to conceive of a process by which individual capitalists pursuing higher profits make decisions that have the result of forcing the overall profit rate lower.

A numerical example of this process may help to explain it. Suppose, for simplicity, that we are in the corn economy of Ricardo; hence there will be only one produced commodity and prices will be proportional to labor values. Suppose further that the value of money is fixed at 1 labor unit per dollar; hence we can translate directly back and forth between money and labor time accounting. Suppose that originally 4/3 units of labor use 1/3 unit of corn as an input to produce 1 unit of new corn; then the labor value of a unit of corn is 2 labor units and the price of corn will be $2.00. Suppose that the wage is $.50 per unit of labor-power; then the workers can buy 1/4 unit of corn with the wage. The total cost of producing 1 unit of corn will be $1.33, half in wages and half in the cost of the corn input. The profit will be $.67; and the profit rate, assuming the rate of turnover to be 1 (that is, capital invested equals the cost), will be 50%.

If an individual capitalist discovers a way to produce a unit of corn with only 1/2 unit of labor but 1/2 unit of corn (that is, increased corn) input, his costs at the going prices will be $.25 for labor and $1.00 for corn input, or $1.25 altogether. Because the going price for corn is $2.00, this capitalist's profit is $.75 per unit of corn on costs of $1.25, for a profit rate of 60%. Because the average rate of profit is only 50%, this profit rate represents a super-profit. The chance to appropriate this super-profit will be a strong incentive for any individual capitalist to adopt this technique of production.

Suppose now that all capitalists have discovered the new method. Then the labor value of corn will have fallen to 1, because 1/2 unit of labor produces a net corn output of 1/2 unit in the new technique. If the value of money remains constant at 1 unit of labor per dollar, the price of corn will fall to $1.00. The costs of a typical producer, with a money wage of $.50, will be $.25 for labor and $.50 for corn input, or $.75 altogether. At a price of $1.00 for corn, this production method gives a profit of $.25 on costs of $.75 and a profit rate of 33.33%, a profit rate even lower than the original profit rate of 50%.

Notice that in this example there is a rise in the real wage between the initial and the final situations. In the final situation the money wage of $.50 buys 1/2 unit of corn rather than the 1/4 unit of corn $.50 could buy originally. Here we have held the rate of surplus value constant at 100%. If the real wage were held constant, the money wage would have to fall to $.25 in the final situation. Then the costs of the typical producer would be $.125 for labor and $.50 for corn input, for a total of $.625 and a profit of $.375 if corn sold at $1.00. At these prices, this production method gives a profit rate of 60%. But notice that in holding the real wage constant we have reduced the value of labor-power from 1/2 to 1/4 and increased the rate of surplus value from 100% to 300%. In this example there could be some fall in the value of labor-power and some rise in the rate of exploitation, with a rising real wage and a falling rate of profit between the initial and the final situations.

Countertendencies to the Falling Rate of Profit (Capital 3.14)

Marx argues that the basic tendency (or the lowest layer of determinations, in the language used in our discussion of Marx's method) in capitalist production is to increase the productivity of labor by substituting nonlabor inputs for labor. As we have seen, this process, if the value of labor-power remains unchanged, can have the effect of lowering the system-wide average rate of profit. But Marx was aware that real historical experience was considerably more complex than this. He expressed the qualifications to this general tendency or law as *countertendencies*, that is, higher level determinations that offset or modify the operation of the basic tendency, a way of arguing that is consistent with the view of theory as a system of layered determinations.

The first countertendency listed by Marx is in fact the possibility that the rate of exploitation may rise as a result of a fall in the value of labor-power with the rising productivity of labor. This possibility has already been analyzed by Marx in his discussion of relative surplus value. Marx was never very explicit in admitting that a constant value of labor-power together with a rising productivity of labor implies a rising real wage. But there is certainly the possibility in real capital accumulation for the basic pattern of rising labor productivity, a rising rate of surplus value, a rising real wage, and a falling rate of profit that seems to be inherent in Marx's analysis.

The second countertendency Marx lists is the depression of wages below the value of labor-power in cases in which capitalists can gain a temporary advantage in their bargaining with workers. As Marx points out, this possibility, however significant it may be in particular historical periods, is at a very different level of abstraction from the other arguments concerning the falling rate of profit.

The third countertendency is considerably more important. It is the fact that the general increase in labor productivity will lower the value and price of elements of constant capital. This effect was taken into account in the example analyzed in the preceding section, because the corn input was valued in the last situation at its new price. If this had not been true, the fall in the rate of profit would have been considerably greater.

The fourth countertendency Marx calls relative overpopulation— the emergence of unemployment as workers are displaced by technical change. In weakening the bargaining power of employed workers, this effect presumably reinforces the possible fall in the real wage discussed in the first countertendency and thus offsets the fall in the rate of profit.

Finally, Marx points out that foreign trade, if it makes available either cheaper elements of constant capital or cheaper means of subsistence, will tend to reduce production costs for capital and sustain the rate of profit.

The picture Marx presents in his full discussion of the falling rate of profit is complex. The basic dynamic, he argues, is the technical progressiveness of capitalism as a mode of production, a progressiveness that leads to constant increases in labor productivity. But because these increases typically involve increases in nonlabor inputs as well, there is a tendency for the average rate of profit to fall if the value of labor-power remains constant. In reality, however, there will be pressures, more or less successful, for the value of labor-power to fall as labor productivity rises, even if the real wage is increasing to some degree. Furthermore, the rise in labor productivity cheapens the elements of constant capital and retards the fall in the rate of profit. The basic tendency for the rate of profit to fall is something like the law of gravity, in the sense that everything tends to fall to the ground. Many things stand up, such as buildings and people, because of offsetting structures or processes. But it is impossible to understand these offsetting structures without understanding the law of gravity itself. In the same way, we may see periods of capital accumulation where the profit rate does not fall very much. If this is true, Marx's analysis leads us to look at what is happening to the value of labor-power and to the value of elements of constant capital for an explanation.

The Inevitability of the Falling Rate of Profit

The status of the tendency for the rate of profit to fall as a universal law of capital accumulation has been questioned by many people, including some Marxists. The most common criticism along these lines argues that Marx fails to establish the necessity or inevitability of the falling rate of profit and thus fails to show that it represents an internal limit or boundary to capital accumulation.

First, is there any reason to think that technical progress under capitalism has to take the form of a substitution of nonlabor inputs for labor inputs? Would not cost-cutting capitalists be just as interested in economizing on nonlabor inputs to production as on labor inputs? Might there not be some kinds of technical change that reduce both labor and nonlabor inputs? Marx's argument depends on the hypothesis that increases in labor productivity involve a fall in the composition of capital outlays, that is, wages become a smaller proportion of the total capital advanced. This fall may occur, but it is hard to see why it should.

Second, as Sweezy (1949, chap. 6) remarks, what is the basis for Marx's categorization of the rise in the rate of exploitation due to technical change as a countertendency? If, as Marx wrote in Volume 1 of *Capital*, the value of labor-power is the labor contained in a historically and morally determined subsistence standard of living, should not rises in labor productivity automatically and inherently involve a fall in the value of labor-power and a rise in the rate of surplus value? This is in fact close to the position Marx takes in Volume 1 when he discusses relative surplus value. If the fall in the value of labor-power is a direct and predictable effect of increases in labor productivity, why is this effect classified as a countertendency rather than as part of the basic tendency itself?

It is possible to imagine technical changes in capitalist society that do not lower the composition of capital outlays. It is also possible to imagine situations (as Marx does in his passage on the countertendencies) in which a rise in the rate of surplus value could offset the tendency for the rate of profit to fall, even when technical change does take the form of lowering the proportion of wages in capital outlays. What is not so clear is whether what Marx wrote was intended to say anything different. The debate over this point touches very difficult questions of language, philosophy, and method. In the Hegelian tradition in which Marx wrote and thought, whatever really happens has a special status and character. It is "necessary" because it is real. In Hegel's *Logic* (1830, pp. 202–208) we find the striking claim that the *possible* becomes the *necessary* in the sense that we first become aware of real cases as contingent possibilities before we understand the full determinations of the reality they explain. It is unlikely that Marx, in using the words *law* or *necessary* meant to suggest that it was possible to deduce the pattern of capital accumulation from some a priori axioms. Such a procedure would be completely at odds with his own account of his method. More likely he meant to claim that it is possible to explain the actual pattern of capital accumulation on rational grounds within the framework of his theory.

The fact that a rise in the rate of surplus value may offset the falling rate of profit is somewhat easier to deal with. In opposition to most later economists, who give a privileged place to the real use-values produced and circulated in the economy, Marx insists on the social importance and relevance of value itself and its distribution. In fact, he often argues as if real use-values were important primarily as vehicles for the distribution of social labor time. What is central in Marx's theory are the social relations into which people enter in order to feed, clothe, and house themselves, not the amount or quality of what they eat, wear, or inhabit. The value of labor-power divides value added between capitalists and workers. It makes good sense from the point of view of the labor theory of value to consider first what happens when the value of labor-power remains constant. Furthermore, changes in the value of labor-power in response to changes in labor productivity are not automatic and involve substantial social and economic conflicts. For the value of labor-power to fall, money wages must fall or the value of money must decline, as the example analyzed earlier makes clear. It does not seem arbitrary to classify cases that depend on these further events in a different category from the change in labor productivity that sets the process in motion.

The Possibility of a Falling Rate of Profit

An even more destructive critique of Marx's theory of the falling rate of profit has been proposed by Okishio (1961). Okishio claims that, on Marx's assumptions, the rate of profit must *rise* in the course of capitalist adoption of new techniques of production. This line of thinking leads to the conclusion that the falling rate of profit is not only not necessary but not even possible within Marx's theoretical framework.

This argument is based on *Okishio's theorem*. Suppose that we begin with a capitalist production system in which capitalists in all sectors achieve the same average rate of profit at existing prices. In considering the possibility of changing to new techniques of production, capitalists will ask themselves whether or not the proposed new technique will yield a super-profit at the existing prices. A super-profit will occur only if the cost of production (equal to capital invested on the assumption that the rate of turnover is one) for the new technique is lower at current prices than that for the existing technique. We shall call techniques that meet this test *viable* because there is an incentive for capitalists to adopt them. Okishio's theorem states that if capitalists adopt a viable technique and if the real wage remains constant, then the new average rate of profit can never be lower than the initial rate. The key assumption in this theorem is that the real wage remains constant after the adoption of the new technique.

It is possible to demonstrate this theorem in very general models of production, but the points at issue can be seen simply in a one-commodity model of production like the corn model outlined in the example given earlier. Suppose that the current technique requires n units of labor and a units of corn to produce 1 unit of corn, that the value of money is 1 unit of labor per dollar, and that the money wage rate is w. The labor value of a unit of corn, which will also be its price, is

$$p = \frac{n}{1-a} \tag{8.1}$$

The real wage must be the amount of corn the money wage can buy at this price,

$$b = \frac{w}{p} = \frac{w[1-a]}{n} \tag{8.2}$$

The profit per unit corn at these prices will be $p - [pa + wn] = p[1-a-bn]$, and the profit rate will be

$$r = \frac{p[1-a-bn]}{[a+bn]} = \frac{1}{a+bn} - 1 \tag{8.3}$$

Suppose now that there is a new technique that requires n' units of labor and a' units of corn to produce 1 unit of corn output. The cost of producing a unit of corn using this technique will be $wn' + pa'$, and the technique will have lower costs than the current technique, that is, will be viable if

$$wn' + pa' < wn + pa \tag{8.4}$$

or, using (8.1) and (8.2), if

$$a' + bn' < a + bn \tag{8.5}$$

Suppose that the new technique is generally adopted. Then the new labor value and price of corn will be

$$p' = \frac{n'}{1-a'} \tag{8.6}$$

and the new wage rate must be

$$w' = p'b \tag{8.7}$$

At this new price and wage rate, the profit on a unit of corn will be $p' - [p'a' + w'n'] = p'[1 - a' - bn']$, and the new profit rate r' will be

$$r = \frac{1}{a' + bn'} - 1 \tag{8.8}$$

Obviously if $a' + bn' < a + bn'$, $r' > r$, and any viable technique will lead to a higher, not a lower, rate of profit. The argument required to establish this proposition when there are many sectors of production is somewhat more mathematically complex, but it rests on the same logic.

We can contrast this proof with what happens if we hold the value of labor-power constant by holding the money wage and the value of money constant. The profit per unit of corn with the original technique is given by $p - pa - wn$, and the rate of profit will be

$$r = \frac{p}{pa + wn} - 1 = \frac{1}{a + [1 - a]w} - 1 \tag{8.9}$$

because $p = n/[1 - a]$, from (8.1).

With the new technique, the profit rate will be

$$r' = \frac{1}{a' + [1 - a']w} - 1 \tag{8.10}$$

Thus if $a' > a$, the new system-wide average rate of profit will fall if the value of labor-power remains constant.

There are many viable new techniques that have $a' > a$, because all that is required is for

$$\frac{n - n'}{a' - a} < \frac{w}{p} \tag{8.11}$$

from (8.5). This was exactly the situation in the example analyzed in the section *Marx's Theory of the Falling Rate of Profit*.

The interest of Okishio's critique of Marx's argument hangs on two issues. First, is it essential for Marx's argument that the real wage be held constant? Second, in real capitalist economies is there a tendency for real wages to be constant in periods of technical change? As we have seen in our discussion of the value of labor-power and of the transformation problem, it was quite natural for Marx to focus his attention on the value of labor-power in the sense of the social labor time workers receive in exchange for a unit of their labor-power rather than on the real wage. Only a very dogmatic reading of the passage in *Capital* (1867, pp. 170–171), in which Marx explains the determination of the real wage by a historically and morally determined standard of living, would support a contrary conclusion.

The Okishio theorem is not very relevant to the experience of real capitalist economies because the characteristic pattern of capital accumulation involves increases in real wages at the same time as the value of labor-power falls and the rate of exploitation rises. Thus real capitalist economies fall into the class of cases in which it is impossible to say a priori whether the process of technical change will raise or lower the profit rate. Only the extremely strong assumption of a constant real wage (that is, that capitalists will appropriate all the fruits of technical progress) can yield Okishio's conclusion.

Conclusion

Marx's investigation of the problem of the falling rate of profit was motivated by the desire to understand the development of real capitalist economies as capital accumulated. The pattern of this development in terms of the basic determinants of capital accumulation can be summarized as follows: (1) a rising productivity of labor; (2) a rising rate of surplus value; (3) a rising real wage; (4) a falling ratio of production wages to total capital outlays; and (5) a falling rate of profit. Marx tried to explain this pattern on the basis of the technical progressiveness of capitalism as a mode of production.

There is such strong empirical support for the first four elements of this pattern that they are hardly controversial. The evidence supporting the conclusion that the rate of profit tends to fall during long periods of capital accumulation is considerably more ambiguous and difficult to interpret.

It is not hard to see why Marx was so interested in this problem, because it leads to a beautiful dialectical denouement. What, says Marx, is the progressive, the historically positive side of capitalism as a mode of production? It is its ability to revolutionize production, to unleash productive forces, and hence to magnify human productive powers. This process involves an attempt to reduce the use of human labor to a minimum. But it is human labor that provides the surplus value that is the rationale for existence of capital. In trying to reduce the labor time required for production, capitalism cuts away its own social basis in unpaid labor time. This contradiction manifests itself in the falling rate of profit. The positive moment of the capitalist mode of production, technical progressivity, brings with it the erosion of the profit rate on which the mode of production rests.

9

The Theory of Capitalist Crisis

The Temporal Unevenness of Capital Accumulation

The picture of capital accumulation presented by the circuit of capital model on a steady-state path is one of smooth, continuous, and balanced growth. All measures of economic activity, flows and stocks of value, are growing at the same rate. Value moves through each phase of the circuit of capital regularly and easily. There is no tendency for finished commodities to pile up unsold in inventories, or for inventories to become depleted, or for money capital to stagnate. If there are changes in the pattern of social consumption, the system is adapting to them smoothly by shifting capital out of declining sectors and into growing sectors. The value of money is constant or changing in a predictable and steady pattern.

History shows few periods of such sustained and even accumulation. Invariably the accumulation process takes place unevenly, with high rates of growth interrupted by periods of slow or negative growth. At certain times inventories of commodities accumulate unsold and excess capacity emerges in productive facilities. The rate of change of the value of money undergoes sharp changes. Typically after a longer or shorter period of such disturbances, the system returns to a mode of steady accumulation, only to be disturbed once more.

A careful study of the historical record shows that these periods of disturbance in capital accumulation have a regular pattern, in that certain events usually precede others in the historical sequence. But the pattern of disturbances is irregular in that the timing of different phases and the intervals between different phases are variable. The magnitudes of the changes in production and other aspects of the circuit of capital also vary widely.

The stylized aspects of disturbances to accumulation are summed up in the notion of the *business cycle*. The cycle begins with the system growing in some approximation of steady accumulation with a stable value of money. This steady growth accelerates into a boom; the value of money starts to fall more rapidly, shortages begin to develop, interest rates rise, and the rate of profit declines. The rapid expansion finally reaches a turning point, often marked by extreme conditions in credit markets (either very high rates of interest or a breakdown in the lending process altogether), after which the rate of growth of output actually becomes negative. In this recession phase capitalists find it difficult to sell the commodities they have produced and cut back on production, thereby creating unemployment and excess capacity. Capital outlays fall; hence money capital tends to stagnate. At some point the contraction phase comes to an end—normally after the value of money becomes more stable or starts to rise and after interest rates fall sharply—and a stronger or weaker phase of accumulation starts again.

Many business cycle movements are mild and short-lived; and it is possible to view them as a normal part of capital accumulation. But at times, as in the 1930s in the world economy, these disturbances are so severe and protracted as to call into question the further development of the capitalist system itself. These severe episodes Marx calls *crises* of the system. They often mark a sharp turning point in the developmental pattern of capitalism, involving major political changes and major changes in the relation of the State to the market.

The General Theory of Crises

Marx often discusses capitalist crises as examples of the general contradictions of capitalist production in extreme conditions. A severe crisis of accumulation dramatically manifests a rapid increase in unfilled need (as unemployment rises and incomes fall) on the one hand and a rapid increase in unused capacity to meet needs (as means of production stand idle and inventories are destroyed) on the other. This irrational pattern Marx viewed as essentially new and specific to capitalist production. Earlier social formations experienced severe productive crises, of course, with famines, floods, epidemics, and wars. But in these situations the increase in unfilled need corresponds to the destruction of means of production. It is not hard to understand why people have unfilled needs when their means of production have been destroyed, but it is a great puzzle why people should experience unfilled need at the same time that a great productive apparatus stands unused. Marx says (1894, pp. 257–258):

> There are not too many necessities of life produced, in proportion to the existing population. Quite the reverse. Too little is produced to decently and humanely satisfy the wants of the great mass.
>
> There are not too many means of production produced to employ the able-bodied portion of the population. Quite the reverse . . .
>
> On the other hand, too many means of labour and necessities of life are produced at times to permit of their serving as means for the exploitation of labourers at a certain rate of profit . . .
>
> Not too much wealth is produced. But at times too much wealth is produced in its capitalistic, self-contradictory forms.

Without going into very much detail as to the exact mechanisms of crisis, Marx argues that this pattern reflects the basic contradiction in commodity production between use-value and value. Commodity production is motivated proximately by the pursuit of value, and capitalist production more specifically by the pursuit of surplus value. The production and distribution of use-values is an incidental by-product of this pursuit of value. In such a system we can see how unfilled need might coexist with unused capacity to produce when for some reason the production of use-values becomes inconsistent with the appropriation or preservation of value.

Marx makes this point in the early pages of *Capital*. In his discussion (1867, pp. 113–114) of the form $C - M - C'$, he emphasizes the separation of sale and purchase that develops along with money and the commodity form. He points out the connection between crisis and the fundamental character of commodity production in the following terms:

> If the interval of time between the two complementary phases of the metamorphosis of a commodity become too great, if the split

between the sale and the purchase become too pronounced, the intimate connection between them, their oneness, asserts itself by producing—a crisis. The antithesis, use-value and value; the contradictions that private labour is bound to manifest itself as direct social labour, that a particularised concrete kind of labour has to pass for abstract human labour; the contradiction between the personification of objects and the representation of persons by things; all these antitheses and contradictions, which are immanent in commodities, assert themselves, and develop their modes of motion, in the antithetical phases of the metamorphosis of a commodity. These modes therefore imply the possibility, and no more than the possibility, of crises. The conversion of this mere possibility into a reality is the result of a long series of relations, that, from our present standpoint of simple circulation, have as yet no existence.

Marx develops this line of argument throughout *Capital*. Once we understand the division of capitalist society between workers and capitalists, the problem of crises can be given a more precise form. The behavior of workers is unlikely to give rise to a severe rupture between sales and purchases because workers would use their stocks of money value to maintain their consumption in the face of a disturbance. If workers had control over the whole flow of value in the system, a severe crisis could not occur. In this sense the restricted purchasing power of the workers is a necessary condition for capitalist crisis. Marx says in *Theories of Surplus Value* (1963, p. 492):

> The criterion of the expansion of production is *capital* itself, the existing level of the conditions of production and the unlimited desire of the capitalists to enrich themselves and to enlarge their capital, but by no means *consumption*, which from the outset is inhibited, since the majority of the population, the working people, can only expand their consumption within very narrow limits, whereas the demand for labour, although it grows *absolutely*, decreases *relatively*, to the same extent as capitalism develops.

The sufficient condition for crisis is the existence of capitalist production itself because capitalists do not sell in order to buy, rather they buy in order to sell. The logic of the pursuit of surplus value contains within itself the problem of crisis. Marx sums up this argument in *Capital* (1894, p. 258):

> the expansion or contraction of production are determined by the appropriation of unpaid labour and the proportion of this unpaid

labour to materialised labour in general, or to speak the language of the capitalists, by profit and the proportion of this profit to the employed capital, thus by a definite rate of profit, rather than the relation of production to social requirements, i.e., to the requirements of socially developed human beings. It is for this reason that the capitalist mode of production meets with barriers at a certain expanded stage of production which, if viewed from the other premise, would reversely have been altogether inadequate. It comes to a standstill at a point fixed by the production and realisation of profit, and not the satisfaction of requirements.

Thus the central point in Marx's general analysis of capitalist crisis is that crisis arises inherently from the contradictions of the capitalist mode of production. Crises are not imposed on the system from outside it but develop with its own development. Furthermore Marx sees crisis as purgative. The crisis tends to resolve the problems that created it and to recreate the conditions for renewed accumulation.

Specific Theories of Crisis

In Marx's available works there is no systematic, synthetic discussion of the theory of capitalist crisis. He discusses this issue in a wide variety of contexts, often as a parenthesis in a discussion of some other issue and frequently in the course of making a critique of some earlier writer. The most sustained discussion of the problem of crisis occurs in *Theories of Surplus Value* (1963, chap. 17); but even in this text Marx's primary aim is to make a thorough critique of Ricardo's discussion of Say's Law, not to put forward a positive theory of the sources of capitalist crisis.

Thus it seems fair to say that in the strict sense there is no Marxist theory of capitalist crisis, no model, that is, that we can reliably view as arising from a fully considered position of Marx himself. Later scholars, polemicists, and revolutionaries have reconstructed a variety of theories of crisis in the strict sense, each one emphasizing one or another aspect of Marx's unsystematic discussion.

There are three broad categories into which these attempted reconstructions fall. First, some theories locate crisis in the *disproportionalities* that arise in the course of capital accumulation. These theories naturally center on the idea of the anarchy of capitalist production within the framework of the two-department analysis of reproduction in Marx's work. Second, an influential group of theories stresses *underconsumption*, or inadequate aggregate demand, as the source of capitalist crisis. The general idea is that the distributional inequities of capitalist relations of production are inconsistent with system-wide requirements for the growth of demand and the realization of the product. Finally, some theories approach the problem through the ideas associated with the law of *the tendency for the rate of profit to fall* with accumulation. In these theories the falling rate of profit has to be converted into a generalized crisis of realization.

Marx's Critique of Say's Law

All these theories of crisis reject, along the lines of Marx's own critique, the classical economic postulate known as *Say's Law*. As we have seen through the analysis of the circuit of capital, if all the commodities produced in a given period could be sold for money at given prices, the resulting money revenues would suffice to buy the commodities at those same prices. Thus there is in a tautological sense a potential money demand for commodities created by their very production. The classical economists who espoused Say's Law went one step further and argued that this potential money demand becomes actual and that the monetary mechanism somehow smoothly and regularly solves the problem of financing these potential money demands.

The simplest arguments for this position eliminate the concept of money altogether and are based on the premise that commodities exchange directly for each other. Mill says, astoundingly enough, "What constitutes the means of payment for commodities is simply commodities" (quoted in Keynes, 1936, p. 18). A more sophisticated line of argument claims that the behavior of economic agents or the operation of markets normally assures that the production of commodities will generate the money demand required to buy them. Ricardo sums up this position (quoted in Marx, 1963, p. 493) by saying, "no man produces, but with a view to consume or sell, and he never sells, but with an intention to purchase some other commodity."

Marx criticized both versions of Say's Law. First, he insists on the importance of the mediation of money in exchange. He says in *Capital* (1867, p. 113):

The sale and purchase constitute one identical act . . . That identity further implies that the exchange, if it do take place, constitutes a period of rest, an interval, long or short, in the life of the commodity . . . No one can sell unless some one else purchases. But no one is forthwith bound to purchase, because he has just sold.

We can use the circuit of capital framework to give more specificity to this idea. In the circuit of capital the time lags in production and spending give rise to stocks of value tied up in productive capital, financial capital, and commercial capital. Suppose that the time lag in capitalist spending of money capital lengthens for some reason. Capital outlays then must fall below their previous level and, as a result, so must sales of commodities. Because production continues on the basis of earlier capital outlays, the immediate effect will be an increase in inventories of finished commodities awaiting sale and a lengthening of the time lag between the production of commodities and their sale. This sequence of events is precisely what happens in that phase of a capitalist crisis in which firms have difficulty selling what they have produced. Thus the scale of aggregate demand in the market in relation to production can vary if capitalists (or workers, for that matter) lengthen the time lag in their spending. This possibility means that there can be insufficient aggregate demand in certain periods, thus contradicting the claim of Say's Law.

Marx goes further than this, however. He argues that capitalist systems will in fact tend to experience such shifts in spending lags and in aggregate demand, whereas other modes of production will not. Thus the phenomenon of crisis is linked to the behavior of producers in a capitalist economy in *Theories of Surplus Value* (1963, pp. 502–503):

> In a situation where men produce for themselves, there are indeec no crises, but neither is there capitalist production. Nor have we ever heard that the ancients, with their slave production ever knew crises, although individual producers among the ancients, too, did go bankrupt.
> . . . The capitalist's immediate object in selling, is to turn his commodity, or rather his commodity capital, back into *money capital*, and thereby to *realise* his profit. Consumption—revenue—is by no means the guiding motive in this process, although it is for the person who only sells *commodities* in order to transform them into means of subsistence. But this is not capitalist production, in which revenue appears as the result and not as the determining purpose.

Everyone *sells* first of all in order to sell, that is to say, in order to transform commodities into money.

The various Marxist theories of crisis differ in their choice of the exact aspect of capitalist production that leads to crisis.

Theories of Disproportionality

Marx's analysis of simple and expanded reproduction points up the necessity for a capitalist economy to allocate capital correctly between the two departments of production. But at the same time Marx argues that capitalist production is characterized by anarchy in precisely the area concerned here, that is, the allocation of social capital. In principle capital is allocated entirely by the decentralized decisions of capitalists. If these decentralized decisions result in too much capital being allocated in one department, the balancing conditions for smooth reproduction will be violated. The overexpanded department will find difficulty in selling its whole output, and its rate of profit will fall relative to the underexpanded market. Could the crisis be the method the system uses to resolve these contradictions?

This story is, of course, the basic theme of the classical economists, especially Smith, in praise of the market system. Imbalances of allocation are supposed to be corrected by the decentralized mechanisms of capital allocation. That is, as profit rates rise in one department relative to the other, capitalists will move their capital away from the overexpanded department and toward the underinvested one in their search for a higher rate of profit. As a result, the classical argument goes, the imbalance will tend to be corrected by precisely the anarchic forces that gave rise to it in the first place.

At this point the Marxist argument takes a different turn. The Marxist theorist of disproportionality argues that the contraction of the overexpanded department is not matched by an expansion of the underinvested department; hence aggregate demand falls during the adjustment process and a crisis of realization occurs in both departments. In this version of the theory excessive investment in one department sets in motion a sequence of events that leads to a fall in aggregate demand and thus triggers off a general crisis in the process of reallocating capital from the overexpanded to the underinvested department.

As discussed in the preceding section, a fall in aggregate demand must involve a change in the rate of turnover of money capital in one or both departments. Another aspect of proportionality in the theory of crisis is the question of distribution of capital among its various forms—money capital, productive capital, and commercial capital. Smooth reproduction of the capitalist system requires the correct allocation of capital both between the two departments and among the forms of aggregate capital. If capitalists slow down the rate of turnover of money capital by refusing to spend it on capital outlays at the normal rate, they reduce workers' incomes and their own demand for means of production and thus reduce aggregate demand. As a result, inventories of finished commodities grow as well; or, to put it another way, the rate of turnover of commercial capital also falls. In this situation both holdings of money and inventories of finished commodities are disproportionately large in relation to productive capital. Marx describes this situation in these terms (1963, p. 494): "Surplus value amassed in the form of money (gold or notes) could only be transformed into capital at a loss. It therefore lies idle as a hoard in the banks or in the form of credit money, which in essence makes no difference at all."

In this version of the disproportionality theory, the initial disturbance—the disproportion between the social capital allocated to Departments I and II—is transformed into a disturbance in the relations of the various forms of capital throughout the system. The symptoms of capitalist crisis then appear—the emergence of unsold inventories, cutbacks in production and employment, and a cumulative fall in aggregate demand.

Underconsumption Theories of Crisis

A striking feature of capitalist crisis is the inability of capitalist producers in general to sell all they can produce. In periods of crisis the aggregate demand of buyers falls short of the aggregate supply. Some Marxist theories of crisis make this the fundamental aspect. The basic idea in these approaches is that the capitalist economy cannot generate enough demand to buy back its own output, either as a general rule or specifically in periods of crisis.

The simplest form of the underconsumptionist theory claims that it is logically impossible for capitalist economies to generate enough aggregate demand. In one form (which, as we have seen in Chapter 5, is fallacious) the argument is that because workers receive only a fraction of the value they create as wages, their consumption demand always falls short of the value produced, thus leaving an excess supply on the market. The fallacy in this simple form of underconsumptionist theory lies in its failure to recognize that the surplus value is also available as incomes of capitalists and capitalist firms, which can support additional demand for output. Marx himself makes this point in his discussion of simple reproduction (1893, pp. 410–411):

> It is sheer tautology to say that crises are caused by the scarcity of effective consumption, or of effective consumers . . . But if one were to attempt to give this tautology the semblance of a profounder justification by saying that the working-class receives too small a portion of its own product and the evil would be remedied as soon as it receives a larger share of it and its wages increase in consequence, one could only remark that crises are always prepared by precisely a period in which wages rise generally and the working-class actually gets a larger share of that part of the annual product which is intended for consumption.

As noted in Chapter 5, the sum of workers' and capitalists' incomes is always exactly the same as the sum of the value produced. When sufficient financing is available, either in stocks of a money commodity or in the expansion of credit, a capitalist system can in principle generate enough aggregate demand to stay on a path of expanded reproduction without an unusual buildup of inventories. The demonstration of this possibility does not, of course, show that aggregate demand will in fact always be large enough. To show this, we would have to investigate the forces determining the decisions of workers and capitalists actually to spend the incomes generated in production. It is traditional in Marxist theory to view workers as prone to spend their entire incomes rapidly; hence the problem of inadequate demand in the Marxist framework centers on the decisions of capitalists to spend surplus value, either to buy means of production to expand production through accumulation or to consume.

Perhaps the most influential discussion along these lines is that of Rosa Luxemburg, who argues that capitalist economies are structurally incapable of generating enough aggregate demand to buy back the whole product (Chapter 5). Luxemburg's argument has two facets. First, she makes use of Marx's analysis of expanded reproduction to emphasize the fact that, in the absence of new production of the money commodity and of new borrowing by capitalist firms, the lag in spending will create a growing gap between supply and demand on a path of expanded reproduction. We examined this problem in Chapter 5 and showed that either the expansion of credit or the production of the money commodity is essential to resolving this problem. But this conclusion shifts the focus of the study of aggregate demand away from distribution proper (that is, the division of value added between workers and capitalists) to the workings of the credit system.

Second, Luxemburg argues that even when capitalists have the incomes to spend and can finance their spending, it is unreasonable to suppose that they will invest enough in expanding the total capital to maintain aggregate demand indefinitely. According to Luxemburg, the ultimate purpose of production in a capitalist economy is to provide goods for consumption by workers. Investment in productive capacity can be justified in the end only as a way of producing consumption goods. But the process of accumulation constantly raises the rate of surplus value and reduces the consumption base on which investment depends. As workers receive a smaller and smaller part of the total value added, their spending on consumption becomes less and less important relative to total production. How, asks Luxemburg, can we imagine that capitalists will continue to invest large sums of money to create productive capacity to meet a shrinking final demand? Surely sooner or later excess capacity will emerge and capitalists will refuse to spend their surplus value to accumulate further. Thus even though they have the incomes to create enough demand, they will not in fact spend them rapidly enough to generate the demand required to buy back the total product.

This argument, which shares many elements with Keynesian theories of stagnation, is not easy to dismiss; but there is something strikingly un-Marxian about the premise that the ultimate aim of capitalist production is workers' consumption. Marx's own formulations tend to the opposite conclusion—that the aim of capitalism is the accumulation of capital, a grand and obsessive project to which workers' consumption is a mere accessory.

The most recent form of the underconsumptionist theory of crisis is the theory of the *political business cycle*. This theory rests not on any supposed inability of capitalist social relations to create adequate aggregate demand but on the inability of a class-divided industrial capitalist society to tolerate high levels of aggregate demand indefinitely. As put forward by Kalecki (1943), this theory argues that the level of aggregate demand in the capitalist economy can be regulated by policy decisions of the State, in particular by policies concerning foreign trade, the State budget, and central bank provision of credit to the economy. Kalecki believes that with the proper manipulation of these policies the State could secure consistently high rates of growth of aggregate demand and, in fact, could in most industrialized countries eliminate the floating reserve army of the unemployed. But the disappearance of the reserve army of the unemployed would eliminate the fear of unemployment among workers and greatly strengthen their bargaining position for wages and working conditions vis-a-vis the capitalists. Thus, Kalecki argues, capitalists would eventually pressure the State to reduce aggregate demand and create a controlled capitalist crisis in order to replenish the reserve army of labor and to discipline workers into a conciliatory frame of mind.

The theory of the political business cycle raises important questions. At a technical level it forces us to consider very carefully why it is that the State has the power to determine aggregate demand and exactly what mechanisms permit the State to defeat the spontaneous movements of market-determined decisions. It further suggests that, were workers to achieve a firm hold on the policies of the State, they could eliminate capitalist crises without eliminating capitalism itself. I suspect that this conclusion would not be congenial to Marx.

Falling Rate of Profit Theories of Crisis

Marx's views emphasize the technically progressive character of capitalist production. As we noted in Chapters 4 and 8, this theme emerges first in his discussion of relative surplus value, where technical progress permits a fall in the value of labor-power despite possible increases in workers' real consumption, and second in his discussion of the tendency for the rate of profit to fall with capitalist development because the increase in the rate of surplus value from relative surplus value creation is offset by increases in the ratio of constant to variable capital. It is tempting to try to ground the theory of crisis in this grand theme of Marx's work, to use the falling rate of profit as an explanation of capitalist crisis. In this perspective crisis is linked decisively with the most fundamental and the historically most progressive aspects of capitalist production—its technical progressiveness and its ability to mobilize enormous productive forces.

At first glance this path seems extremely promising. We have seen that capitalist crisis involves a slowing of capitalist spending. It seems quite plausible that a fall in the average rate of profit could produce exactly such a fall in capital outlays. But a closer analysis reveals some deep questions about this argument. Notice that, on the basis of the circuit of capital analysis, continued accumulation is possible at any positive rate of profit, no matter how small it may be in absolute terms. A lower rate of profit certainly implies a lower growth rate for the system of capitals as a whole, given the rate of turnover of productive capital, money capital, and commercial capital and the proportion of surplus value that is reinvested in capitalist production. But a lower absolute rate of growth of the capitalist system does not carry with it any obvious problems for the internal consistency of that system. If the rate of profit were indeed falling consistently, why would the capitalist system not adapt to this fall through a gradual reduction in the rate of accumulation? Such a gradual reduction might not be welcome to capitalists, but it is not obvious that it must lead to the characteristic phenomena of capitalist crisis that we examined earlier. In other words, this explanation for capitalist crisis has to produce some systematic reason why a fall in the rate of profit leads at certain moments to sharp and discontinuous adjustments in economic activity.

But if we grant that such a mechanism (though Marx does not suggest one explicitly) exists in capitalist economies, perhaps involving the credit system and finance, then we also face the problem of specifying which factors produce the fall in the rate of profit and thus are the ultimate causes of the crisis. Here two schools of thought contend. Some scholars, following Ricardo's thinking about the profit rate, emphasize the idea that rising real wages reduce the rate of surplus value and in this way lower the rate of profit. For example, some twentieth-century analysts emphasize the tendency for profit margins to fall near the peak of a boom and for money wages to rise more rapidly than money prices when employment becomes very high. In this view, the boom phase of the business cycle comes to an end because accumulation exhausts the reserve army of labor and as a result competition for jobs becomes much less severe; hence wages rise. The result is a *profit squeeze*, in which the rate of surplus value falls and the profit rate declines. The crisis creates mass unemployment and thus replenishes the reserve army of labor. Competition for jobs increases and wage increases moderate as a result. After some time these processes restore the level of rates of surplus value and profitability and permit accumulation to resume. As we noted earlier, Marx argued that crises were usually preceded by periods of high and rising wages. But in another discussion in *Capital* (1867, p. 620) he argues that it is a mistake to see rising wages as the cause of crises: "To put it mathematically: the rate of accumulation is the independent, not the dependent, variable; the rate of wages, the dependent, not the independent, variable."

In contrast, other writers, while not disputing the empirical importance of the exhaustion of the reserve army of labor at the peak of some booms, emphasize the more classically Marxian idea that the accumulation process itself changes technology and tends to increase the value of constant capital more rapidly than it increases the value of variable capital. In this approach accumulation is seen as gradually altering the technological base of production by increasing the capital investment required to produce. Marx describes this process in these terms in *Capital* (1894, pp. 250–251): "A drop in the rate of profit is attended by a rise in the minimum capital required by an individual capitalist for the productive employment of labour; required both for its exploitation generally, and for making the consumed labour-time suffice as the labour-time necessary for the production of the commodities, so that it does not exceed the average social labour-time required." At some point this cumulative change becomes inconsistent with the profit plans capitalists have made in undertaking investments, and the result is a crisis. The crisis in this view is purgative because it involves the destruction of old capital, an event that raises the average productivity of labor and permits accumulation to resume, albeit at a lower average rate of profit.

Long-Run Tendencies of Capital Accumulation

Marx's discussion of crisis in the sense of short-term disturbances in the process of capital accumulation is accompanied by a discussion of the long-run tendencies of capital accumulation. This analysis has been very influential politically and is among the most controversial of Marx's economic ideas.

Marx argues that the accumulation of capital will be accompanied by dramatic increases in the scale of individual capitals. Two mechanisms are responsible for these increases. First, each capital tends to grow through the reinvestment of its own profits. Thus every successful capital tends to become larger through time. Marx calls this process the *concentration* of capital. Second, Marx argues that large, successful capitals tend to absorb smaller capitals in the course of competition. This tendency corresponds to the phenomena of bankruptcy, merger, and acquisition in contemporary capitalist economies. This process, which Marx calls the *centralization* of capital, can be greatly accelerated by periods of general economic crisis, because many small and weak capitals are put in a vulnerable position by the failure of demand and low profitability characteristic of the crisis.

The processes of concentration and centralization of capital lead to a situation in which the typical important capital is quite large in relation to its competitors and the market, a situation Marx calls *monopoly*. This situation is not monopoly in the strict sense that there is only one seller in a market but monopoly in the larger sense that the capitals have and can use market power (pricing and advertising strategies) as weapons in the competitive struggle.

Capital accumulation also has an important impact on the lives of the working class. First, Marx argues, growth of capital and of employment for some parts of the population will be accompanied by growth in the reserve armies of workers. The rapid pace of technical change constantly displaces employed workers into the ranks of the temporarily unemployed, the floating reserve army. As agriculture becomes organized on capitalist lines, agricultural workers are displaced, forming a great latent reserve army of labor for urban industry. Finally, more and more workers find their skills made obsolete or become discouraged with the struggle for employment and fall into the stagnant reserve army. Although these reserve armies may be diminished in periods of great prosperity, when the demand for labor is very high, they tend to grow along with the accumulation of capital.

Second, according to Marx capital accumulation impoverishes

workers by transforming work itself, dividing tasks into smaller and more routine parts, and thus fragmenting the worker's humanity. The worker collectively controls larger and more powerful means of production, but individually becomes a powerless drudge. The worker is caught between the increasingly sterile and limited work offered by capitalist employers and the competition of the reserve armies of labor that threaten her standard of living.

Third, Marx argues that the progress of capital accumulation depends on constantly rising rates of exploitation, so that productive workers, even when their real wage and standard of living are rising, control a smaller and smaller proportion of the social product. The social gap between the worker and capitalist widens continually with capital accumulation, even when the standards of living of both are rising.

Thus the picture of highly developed capitalism we get from Marx's writings emphasizes the competition of a small number of extremely large capitalist enterprises, each wielding massive economic resources and using advertising, marketing, acquisitions, and financial manipulation in an attempt to gain competitive advantage. In Marx's view such a system of monopoly capital would greatly exacerbate the social contradictions inherent in capitalist society. A small number of very powerful economic decision makers, their decisions aimed at the acquisition of surplus value rather than directly at any social good, would structure and control the social and economic environments. Individual workers, despite the fact that their labor actually created this society, would find themselves left out of significant decisions, living a life very different from that of the elite who controlled the large capitals—in fact, in a different world.

The Ultimate Crisis of Capitalism

Marx also expected this system of monopoly capitals to prepare the way for the transformation of the capitalist economic system into a socialist one. This is a complex conception and has several facets. First of all, the development of monopoly capital rationalizes production on a social basis. Huge productive forces are brought into action by monopoly capital to supply mass demand cheaply. Thus monopoly capital creates the institutions necessary to govern social production on a centralized and social basis. Second, monopoly capitalism creates the technical basis for socialism by developing highly productive technology that enables the production of comfortable social surpluses. Finally, the monopoly stage of capitalism, according to Marx, creates the social and political basis for the emergence of socialism by fostering the development of a massive, conscious, and politically organized working class. This proletarian class Marx sees as the political foundation of a socialist society, as the class that can inherit the direction of the society from capitalists.

The final crisis of capitalism is not so much a technical problem of credit or aggregate demand as it is a human and historic turning point. The final crisis of capitalism arises when capitalism itself actually creates a mass of people who have the technical knowledge and self-confidence to deploy the massive powers of social production for social ends.

10

Socialism

Socialism and the Critique of Capitalism

One of the most puzzling things about the study of Marx's economics is that his writings overwhelmingly consist of a detailed critique of capitalism even though his motivation is to promote the cause of socialism. This puzzle is compounded by the fact that Marx never wrote a systematic and detailed description of what he meant by socialism, although scattered through his writings are passing comments and references to socialist economic practice and substantial critiques of other writers' conceptions of socialism. An understanding of the reasons why Marx does not simply state his plan for socialism and try to persuade the reader of its superiority to capitalism makes it easier to comprehend what Marx wrote about economics.

Marx was impressed and intrigued by the fact that people in different times and places organized themselves to produce the material aspects of their lives in dramatically different ways. His study of the anthropological and historical scholarship available led Marx to emphasize the tremendous differences in technological practice observable in recorded history and the equally great differences in forms of social and political organization. Marx saw as the main tasks of social science and social criticism the description of these characteristic patterns of technology and organization and the discovery of the process by which people changed from one *mode of production,* as he called these patterns, to another.

The people involved in these great transformations have not always been fully conscious of this aspect of their lives' actions. The changes that were dramatically apparent to Marx from the vantage point of the nineteenth century in many cases took centuries to mature in historical reality and were the product of numerous, widely diffused changes in individual behavior. We cannot find in history any single moment when an individual or group of individuals made a conscious decision to alter the mode of production. But it is equally clear that the mode of production changes as large numbers of people gradually come to share a new vision of what human life is and how it ought to be organized. This vision itself changes and matures as parts of it are realized and as the ambiguities and problems inherent in it become more apparent. Marx explains this in a famous, though very controversial, passage (1859, pp. 20–21):

> In the social production of their existence, men inevitably enter into definite relations, which are independent of their will, namely relations of production appropriate to a given stage in the development of their material forces of production. The totality of these relations of production constitutes the economic structure of society, the real foundation, on which arises a legal and political superstructure and to which correspond definite forms of social consciousness. The mode of production of material life conditions the general process of social, political and intellectual life. It is not the consciousness of men that determines their existence, but their social existence that determines their consciousness. At a certain stage of development, the material productive forces of society come into conflict with the existing relations of production or—this merely expresses the same thing in legal terms—with the property relations within the framework of which they have operated hitherto. From forms of development of productive forces these relations turn into their fetters. Then begins an era of social revolution. The changes in the economic foundation lead sooner or later to the transformation of the whole immense superstructure.

Marx saw socialism in this context—as a new mode of production developing on a historical scale. When we see the issues in this light, we can see why an attempt to give a full-blown account of socialism as a mode of production would be inappropriate. We can also see that the discussion of capitalism and socialism cannot be posed in terms of asking what form of organization of production is universally best for people. Certain things are possible for some people, because of their knowledge of themselves and the world, but are impossible for other people who have not made the same discoveries. The same institution may have different effects depending on the context of other institutions within which it exists. For example, an egalitarian mode of distribution may condemn a technologically backward society to stagnation, by making the accumulation of social surplus product impossible. But the same mode of distribution may permit a technologically advanced society to realize possibilities of great social productivity by eliminating certain sources of conflict. Thus the idea of a single "best" mode of social organization of production is incoherent in a historical perspective.

What is appropriate from this point of view is to recognize that modern people, precisely because they have so much more knowledge of their own historical situation, can be much more conscious of the fact that their actions are changing the mode of production. For such a person a clear and accurate critical account of the existing social organization of production is a valuable resource. This is why Marx devoted great effort to clarifying and demystifying the nineteenth-century's knowledge of its own ways of doing things.

From Marx's critique of capitalism we can expect to learn the answers to the following questions about socialism: What aspects of capitalist economic organization is it possible to change? What connections are there between different institutions in the capitalist economy such that change in one institution requires changes in others if it is not to be self-defeating? What social functions do the arrangements of capitalist economies perform, and hence what provisions will a socialist economy have to make to accomplish these same functions? What aspects of capitalism will socialism have to incorporate if it is to be a historical advance over capitalist production?

The Positive Aspects of Capitalism

Marx had a two-sided attitude toward capitalism. In relation to those modes of production that preceded it, Marx saw capitalism as a decisive step forward in human history and emancipation. In *Capital* (1894, p. 819) he remarks:

Surplus-labour in general, as labour performed over and above the given requirements, must always remain. In the capitalist as well as in the slave system, etc., it merely assumes an antagonistic form and is supplemented by complete idleness of a stratum of society . . . It is one of the civilising aspects of capital that it enforces this surplus-labour in a manner and under conditions which are more advantageous to the development of the productive forces, social relations, and the creation of the elements for a new and higher form than under the preceding forms of slavery, serfdom, etc.

But in relation to the possible future that capitalism has founded, Marx saw capitalism as regressive, limited, and destined to perish because of its own contradictions.

Considerable insight into Marx's ideas about socialism can be gained from an examination of those aspects of capitalism that Marx identifies as positive, because he sees socialism as inheriting and improving upon those features of capitalism. For Marx, capitalism achieves an important emancipation of people individually and internally and a corresponding improvement in their ability to marshal their energies in social production. The capitalist as a personality accepts the power and responsibility of constructing the material world through his or her own actions and decisions. The capitalist does not take the world as a given environment but as a medium for his own actions to transform and improve. This matter-of-fact materialism, hostile to superstition, tradition, and taboo and restlessly seeking instruments to achieve its ends, is very attractive to Marx. In the *Communist Manifesto* (Marx and Engels, 1848, p. 38) we read:

> The bourgeoisie cannot exist without constantly revolutionising the instruments of production, and thereby the relations of production, and with them the whole relations of society. Conservation of the the old modes of production in unaltered form, was, on the contrary, the first condition of existence for all earlier industrial classes. Constant revolutionising of production, uninterrupted disturbance of all social conditions, everlasting uncertainty and agitation distinguish the bourgeois epoch from all earlier ones. All fixed, fast-frozen relations, with their train of ancient and venerable prejudices and opinions, are swept away, all new-formed ones become antiquated before they can ossify. All that is solid melts into air, all that is holy is profaned, and man is at last compelled to face with sober senses, his real conditions of life, and his relations with his kind.

Corresponding to this subjective state of mind is the capitalist's ability to mobilize enormous social energies for production and to set in motion the constant innovation and technical change characteristic of capitalist society. Marx returns again and again to the theme of the technically progressive character of capitalist production; it is at the heart of this most controversial and hard-won insights, such as relative surplus value and the tendency for the rate of profit to fall. This technical progressiveness gives capitalism the power to mobilize social surpluses on a scale unimaginable to people of earlier eras.

Marx envisions a socialism that adopts these two central, positive elements of capitalism. Socialist people will presumably also be matter-of-fact materialists. They will consciously accept human responsibility for the construction of the human world, scorning the refuge of theological excuses for human failure. Equally important, they will share with capitalists the power to mobilize social energy on a large scale and also to dispose of a massive social surplus product. Thus Marx's socialism has nothing nostalgic about it; he is not interested in a return to small-scale production or in the abandonment of advanced technology, but in the aggressive and instrumental use of scale and technique in pursuit of social ends.

The Negative Aspects of Capitalism

If Marx accepted scale and technology, two of the most dramatic manifestations of modern capitalism, what was it that he did not like about it? For Marx the fundamental limitation of capitalism was the contradiction that the capitalists wield their tremendous social power on the basis of a private, rather than a social, principle and as a result can never achieve the social possibilities they open up. The capitalists' matter-of-fact materialism is construed within the framework of individualism. Viewed objectively the capitalist is the agent of social production and social change, but the capitalist subjectively sees himself or herself as locked in a private and individual struggle for success and survival. The successful capitalist constantly threatens to transcend these individual limits, by organizing and rationalizing production on a social basis; but the limits of the system reassert themselves by frustrating the full accomplishment of this goal. As capitalism enlarges the scale and advances the technology of social production, more and more social possibilities are frustrated by the need to retain and shore up the private and competitive basis of the system. Again, in the *Communist Manifesto* Marx and Engels explain this view (1848, pp. 40–41):

> Modern bourgeois society with its relations of production, of exchange and of property, a society that has conjured up such gigantic means of production and exchange, is like the sorcerer, who is no longer able to control the powers of the nether world whom he has called up by his spells . . . The productive forces at the disposal of society no longer tend to further the development of the conditions of bourgeois property; on the contrary, they have become too powerful for these conditions, by which they are fettered, and so soon as they overcome these fetters, they bring disorder into the whole of bourgeois society, endanger the existence of bourgeois property. The conditions of bourgeois society are too narrow to comprise the wealth created by them.

It seems, then, that the heart of Marx's critique of capitalism as a mode of production centers on the concept of commodity fetishism. The great weakness of capitalism in this view is that the commodity relation prevents people from understanding clearly how their own actions produce their material and social existence. In *Capital* (1894, p. 826) he says: "We have already pointed out the mystifying character that transforms the social relations, for which the material elements of wealth serve as bearers in production, into properties of these things themselves (commodities) and still more pronouncedly transforms the production relation itself into a thing (money)."

Marx aims at a socialism that does away with the commodity form of production and money as the primary vehicles for the organization of social production. This is a powerful and distinctive position. It separates Marx sharply from those people who aim at a redistribution of power and material wealth within the framework of money and commodity production.

Marx's critique of capitalism is also sharply separated from the complaint that capitalist relations of production are immoral. Marx viewed morality as a human creation and, as such, subject to historical development and change. Each historical epoch enunciates its own understanding of the limits of human relationships within its own construction of those relations. In a slave society, for example, the standards of moral behavior of slaveowners toward slaves are quite different from those of slaveowners toward one another. This distinction is meaningless and abhorrent to a society that has rid itself of slavery. In the *Communist Manifesto* (1848, p. 49) Marx and Engels chide the bourgeoisie:

> The selfish misconception that induces you to transform into eternal laws of nature and of reason, the social forms springing from your present mode of production and form of property—historical relations that rise and disappear in the progress of production—this misconception you share with every ruling class that has preceded you. What you see clearly in the case of ancient property, what you admit in the case of feudal property, you are of course forbidden to admit in the case of your own bourgeois form of property.

What meaning, then, could we give to the idea that capitalism is an immoral mode of production? Certainly the behavior of individuals in capitalist society may contradict the moral standards of capitalism itself; but this is true of any human society. Certainly the moral standards that develop under capitalism may call into question some of the human relations on which capitalism rests; but this, too, is true of any mode of production. From the point of view of nascent socialism some of the fundamental relations necessary to the existence of capitalism, such as the exploitation of wage laborers, may seem immoral and abhorrent, just as the institutions of slavery seem immoral and abhorrent from the point of view of liberal capitalism. But to assert this is simply to take the side of nascent socialism in its historical struggle with capitalism, to adopt the morality of socialism as well as its historical mission. Thus the immorality of capitalism is not a firm base for historical criticism.

For Marx the issue of socialism is primarily a question not of a desirable reform designed to bring social reality into closer correspondence with some moral ideal but of a painful necessity imposed on people by the very success of capitalist development. To realize the possibilities of social production opened up by capitalism, the private basis of control over social surplus will have to be transcended.

From this basic contradiction between the social character of capitalist production and the private basis of capitalist power flow, in Marx's view, the other chief social ills of capitalism. The private character of economic control means that capitalism cannot function except by depriving some part of the population of participation in the fruits of social production, that is, by creating and maintaining the reserve armies of labor. This inherent unevenness in capitalist production creates and recreates the grotesque extremes of human fate experienced by people who organize themselves to produce through capitalist relations of production.

Marx's Critique of Other Visions of Socialism

Even though Marx did not produce a systematic account of his own idea of socialism, he did write extensive critiques of other people's socialist plans. In fact, the work that eventually became *Capital* appears to have begun as a critique of socialist proposals for a labor–money economy, in which certificates received for labor performed would circulate as money. This critique, in the Chapter on Money of the *Grundrisse* (Marx, 1939), centers on the contradiction between the commodity form of production and the socialist goals of this proposal. Marx argues that if a bank were to issue labor certificates it would have to buy all the commodities produced initially in order to sell them back in exchange for the certificates. But then this bank, as a universal buyer and seller, would have to set the prices for commodities produced and in this way replace the market. Marx continues (1939, p. 155):

> [The bank] would have to determine the labour time in which commodities could be produced, with the average means of production available in a given industry . . . But that also would not be sufficient. It would not only have to determine the time in which a certain quantity of products had to be produced, and place the producers in conditions which made their labour equally productive . . . but it would also have to determine the amounts of labour time to be employed in the different branches of production. The latter would be necessary because, in order to realize exchange value and make the bank's currency really convertible, social production in general would have to be stabilized and arranged so that the needs of the partners in exchange were always satisfied . . . Precisely seen, then, the bank would be not only the general buyer and seller, but also the general producer.

Marx concludes that the attempt to reform commodity production by a labor certificate system implies a full socialization of production under central direction.

From this discussion we can see that Marx's conception of socialism involved a fundamental change in the framework of institutions that organize production. The organization and supervision of work cannot be entrusted to the spontaneous, decentralized, and narrowly self-interested interactions of individuals.

Marx also criticizes socialist visions that put an excessive emphasis on the idea of equal distribution of the social product as the essence of socialism. For Marx the aim of an "equal" distribution seems to have appeared as a contradictory and misleading slogan. In the *Critique of the Gotha Programme* (1875, p. 324) Marx comments on the proposal that all workers should share equally in the distribution of the product:

> This *equal* right is an unequal right for unequal labor . . . it tacitly recognises unequal individual endowment and thus productive capacity as natural privileges. *It is, therefore, a right of inequality, in its content, like every right.* Right by its very nature can consist only in the application of an equal standard; but unequal individuals (and they would not be different individuals if they were not unequal) are measurable only by an equal standard in so far as they are brought under an equal point of view, are taken from one *definite* side only, for instance, in the present case, are regarded *only as workers* and nothing more is seen in them, everything else being ignored. Further, one worker is married, another not; one has more children than another, and so on and so forth. Thus, with an equal performance of labour, and hence an equal share in the social consumption fund, one will in fact receive more than another, one will be richer than another, and so on. To avoid all these defects, right instead of being equal would have to be unequal.

Furthermore, in the same text (1875, p. 322) Marx rejects the idea that socialism could mean that workers would receive claims to the whole value of the product as individuals:

> the cooperative proceeds of labour are the *total social product.*
>
> From this must now be deducted:
>
> *First,* cover for replacement of the means of production used up.
>
> *Secondly,* additional portion for expansion of production.
>
> *Thirdly,* reserve or insurance funds to provide against accidents, dislocations caused by natural calamities, etc . . .
>
> Before this is divided among the individuals, there has to be deducted again, from it:

> First, the general costs of administration not belonging to produc-
> tion . . .
> Secondly, that which is intended for the common satisfaction of needs,
> such as schools, health services, etc . . .
> Thirdly, funds for those unable to work . . .

For Marx socialist society must mobilize social surpluses, in order
to defray expenses of administration, welfare, defense, education,
and investment in means of production. This implies that individual workers could not claim the whole product without deduction.

Marx's Conception of Socialism

From these indirect indications we can reconstruct some important aspects of Marx's positive conception of socialism. He saw
socialism as an epochal, historical phenomenon, a pervasive transformation of the relations between people and their subjective
understanding of their situation. This transformation touches the
most fundamental aspects of the organization of production and
people's assumptions about the conditions of their existence. It
requires ultimately the replacement of the spontaneous, decentralized, market-regulated system of commodity production by a
conscious, socially oriented governance of production.

Although this vision is antithetical to many aspects of capitalist
society, Marx saw socialism as transcending and incorporating
many of the positive features of capitalism. As we have seen, the
secular, practical mental set of capitalism is an indispensable part
of socialist society. The mobilization of productive resources and
the deployment of large social surpluses are also common to Marx's
understanding of capitalism and his vision of socialism.

This notion of socialism as incorporating and transcending capitalist institutions extends to the problem of property. For Marx
socialism means, not the abolition of property as an institution
controlling people's access to what they have produced, but the
transformation of certain classes of property into social property,
governed on an explicitly social basis. Marx viewed capitalist
property as the end point of a long process of historical evolution
itself. In his view this evolutionary process would continue and
lead to the development of social forms of property.

Marx's characteristic way of referring to socialist relations of
production was in the phrase "the free association of workers." In

the first chapter of *Capital,* for example (1867, p. 78), Marx describes "a community of free individuals, carrying on their work with the means of production in common, in which the labour-power of all the different individuals is consciously applied as the combined labour-power of the community." Later in Volume 3 of *Capital* (1894, p. 820) Marx returns to this idea:

> Just as the savage must wrestle with Nature to satisfy his wants, to maintain and reproduce life, so must civilised man, and he must do so in all social formations and under all possible modes of production. With his development this realm of physical necessity expands as a result of his wants; but, at the same time, the forces of production which satisfy these wants also increase. Freedom in this field can only consist in socialised man, the associated producers, rationally regulating their interchange with Nature, bringing it under their common control, instead of being ruled by it as by the blind forces of Nature; and achieving this with the least expenditure of energy and under conditions most favourable to, and worthy of, their human nature.

These telegraphic formulations have three important moments. First, production in such a community is organized and directed socially. The authority that governs production and the disposition of social labor is immediately and explicitly social. Its legitimation comes from its representing the community as a whole.

Second, the motivation of individuals for entering into the social labor process is quite different from that of wage-laborers. Whereas the wage-laborer sells her labor-power with the aim of personal survival or advance in the competitive struggle, the socialist worker gives her labor as a part of the grand mosaic of social labor and works to ensure the survival and development of the society as a whole. This change in the social psychology of work is one of the most radical and profound of Marx's ideas.

Finally, the word *conscious* plays a very important role in this passage. For Marx, socialist labor will be based on a massive advance in human understanding. Each member of a community of freely associated producers understands in some appropriate sense the whole system, its history, its goals, and the member's own place in that pattern. Thus an important aspect of socialism for Marx is to dispel the confusion and distortion of commodity fetishism. The historical advance of humanity is, for him, the development of the individual's consciousness.

The Construction of Socialism and the Working Class

The evolution of socialism out of the contradictory forms of capitalist production is in Marx's view the particular task of the working class. Thus Marx addresses his critique of capitalism to workers. At first workers in a capitalist society do not recognize their position in the whole system of production but bear the consciousness and the ethnic and religious identities of their origins. The rigorous experience of capitalist production, according to Marx, will convince workers that they share a single struggle against capitalist employers and ultimately against capitalist production.

This conflict initially appears in the workers' efforts to limit exploitation by shortening the working day, restricting the use of family labor, and raising wages. Marx argues that these goals are only defensive and that any victories workers win in these arenas are inherently transitory. The goal of Marx's analysis is to convince workers that they must move beyond these defensive strategies to an offensive, revolutionary movement to take State power and use it to transform capitalist production into socialism. By taking part in the conflicts over wages, conditions of work, and the length of the working day, workers come to realize that they have problems not as individuals but as a class. In Marx's view this realization is the first step toward understanding that workers as a class can transform the relations of production altogether.

Summary

Marx conceives of socialism as a historical phenomenon, practically arising from capitalism. It is to be approached not primarily in the spirit of planning and calculation but in the spirit of understanding a complex phenomenon that is already in the course of its development.

Because socialism stems historically from the contradictions of capitalist production, the best way to start when attempting to understand it is with a study of these contradictions themselves. Furthermore, the nature of socialism as it eventually develops will be influenced by its origins in capitalist production. Socialism transcends and incorporates capitalist society and capitalist property.

The important functions of capitalism, especially its ability to sustain large-scale production, to mobilize large social surpluses, and to provide systematically for the expansion and technical improvement of production, must be discharged in socialist societies as well. But capitalism achieves these ends in a confused and mystified way, through the form of commodity production and money. These forms distort and hide the true, social nature of production from the individuals who make up capitalist society. These distortions ultimately prevent capitalism from realizing the possibilities it has created.

The transformation of social production to socialist production, then, requires parallel transformations of the organization of production and of the psychology of producers. The social organization of production must be in a position to direct productive efforts from a position of acknowledged legitimacy and practical competence. In a parallel way, the individual producer must choose to contribute his or her labor as part of the emerging social pattern and must be able to see transparently what that pattern is and how individual labor fits into it.

Suggested Readings
References
Index

Suggested Readings

1. On Reading Marx: Method

An indispensable source for understanding Marx's own view of his method is the Introduction to the *Grundrisse* (Marx, 1859, pp. 188–217; 1939, Introduction).

A very helpful discussion of these issues can be found in Rubin (1972, chaps. 1–3) and in Sweezy (1949, chap. 1).

Those interested in more extensive discussions of these problems may sample Rosdolsky (1977, chaps. 2, 34), Avineri (1968, chaps. 1–6), Althusser and Balibar (1970, chaps. 6–9), Lichtheim (1964, pt. 4), Meek (1956, pp. 299–318), or Godelier (1975) for a taste of an enormous literature.

2. The Commodity: Labor, Value, Money

The most compact statement of Marx's thought on these fundamental and difficult issues is in *Capital* 1.1–3. It is also illuminating to read the *Contribution to the Critique of Political Economy* (1859), which is a first and somewhat lengthier treatment of this same material. The Chapter on Money in the *Grundrisse* (1939) is an even earlier and more discursive development of the basic ideas and clarifies many points that are ambiguous in the concise exposition found in *Capital*.

Three texts that clarify the exposition of this material are those by Sweezy (1949, chaps. 2, 3), Rubin (1972, chaps. 6–7, 13–16), and Meek (1956, chaps. 4–6). Rubin is particularly helpful on the concepts of abstract, necessary, and social labor.

A powerful summary of the sweep of Marx's approach to the labor theory of value is contained in Uno (1980).

The problems raised by Marx's theory of money and the concept of the value of money are discussed in de Brunhoff (1967, pt. 1) and Foley (1982, 1983a).

3. The Theory of Capital and Surplus Value

The basic presentation of Marx's theory of surplus value and capitalist production is found in *Capital 1.4–10*.

A useful expository guide to this text is given by Sweezy (1949, chap. 4).

The analysis of social reproduction raises issues of particular importance to feminists, as Hartman and Markusen (1980) and Sen (1980) explain.

4. Production under Capitalism

Marx's discussions of absolute and relative surplus value in Parts 3–5, Volume 1 of *Capital* (especially *1.7–8, 1.9.1, 1.10.1, 1.11–13, 1.14.1, 4–5, 1.15.1–5, 1.16,* and *1.18*) contain some of his most penetrating historical analysis.

The modern literature on these problems is large and fertile. Two starting points are Braverman (1974, especially the Introduction and chaps. 1–6 and 11–14) and Edwards (1979). Schumpeter (1939) develops the issues around the effects of capital on innovation and technique. The problem of the relation of the capitalist to the development of production technology is the subject of Marglin's stimulating two-part essay (1974, 1975).

5. The Reproduction of Capital

Marx's general conception of reproduction is set forth in *Capital 1.23–25*. It is also helpful to read *Capital 2.1* and *2.7* in this context.

Marx treats the relation between the value of labor-power and the concept of the wage in *Capital 1.19*.

The analysis of reproduction that contains Marx's famous schemes of reproduction can be found in *Capital 2.18, 20–21*. Chapter 20, on simple reproduction, is particularly clear and well worked out.

A good commentary on Marx is Sweezy (1949, chap. 5).

Foley (1983b) and Harris (1972) introduce more sophisticated modern treatments of Marx's problem.

Luxemburg (1913, chaps. 1–6, 27–32) has had an important political and theoretical impact.

Kalecki (1971) and Steindl (1952) have developed Marx's approach into a powerful and novel method of analyzing the dynamics of the capitalist economy.

Other interesting comments on these problems can be found in Rosdolsky (1977, pp. 63–72 and chaps. 11–24), Levine (1975), and de Brunhoff (1967, pt. 2, chap. 1).

6. The Equalization of the Rate of Profit

Marx treats the formation of the rate of profit in *Capital 3.1–4*, and his solution to the transformation problem is in *Capital 3.8–10*.

The later literature on this problem is enormous. Sweezy (1949, chap. 7) puts forward the traditional approach and critique of Marx's solution clearly.

The traditional correction of Marx, which holds workers' consumption constant but does not preserve the quantity of surplus value, is explained by Morishima (1973) and Medio (1972). Steedman (1977) develops the critique of the labor theory of value on the basis of this interpretation. Fine and Harris (1979, chap. 2) survey this literature and give more extensive references.

The solution that preserves surplus value is presented by Dumenil (1980), Lipietz (1982), and Foley (1982). An important interpretation of Marx's conception of the problem can be found in Baumol (1974).

Other interesting discussions, linking the transformation problem to larger issues in Marx's thought, are to be found in Rubin (1972, chaps. 17–18), Rosdolsky (1977, chap. 25), and Harris (1978, chap. 3).

7. The Division of Surplus Value

Marx discusses the theory of rent in *Capital*, Volume 3, Part VI. The kernel of his argument can be found in Chapters 37 and 38 of the same volume. On the theory of rent, see also Sraffa (1960, chap. 11).

Marx's discussion of interest and finance takes up Part V in Volume 3, *Capital*. Some of these chapters are very incomplete drafts, but Chapters 21–25 carry a consistent and coherent argument.

The problems of productive and unproductive labor are treated by Marx in relation to his discussion of commercial capital in *Capital*, Volume 3, Part IV. Chapter 16 is of particular interest. A good commentary on this problem can be found in Fine and Harris (1979, chap. 3).

Further pursuit of these ideas might start with de Brunhoff (1967, pt. 2, chap. 2) and Mandel (1968, chaps. 7–8).

Wolff (1986) provides a thorough discussion of the theory and measurement of unproductive labor.

8. The Falling Rate of Profit

Marx treats the problem of the falling rate of profit systematically in *Capital* 3.13–15. It is important to see the connection between this discussion and his discussion of relative surplus value in *Capital* 1.12–15.

A helpful summary of the problem and the controversial aspects of Marx's treatment can be found in Sweezy (1949, chap. 6), Fine and Harris (1979, chap. 4), and Meek (1976).

The theme of capitalist innovation leading to super-profits as the mechanism behind technical change is developed eloquently by Schumpeter (1939).

The arguments supporting the Okishio position that it is impossible for the rate of profit to fall unless the real wage also rises are developed by Roemer (1977) and van Parijs (1980), who also give extensive references to the other contributions to this line of thinking. Bowles (1981) also explains Okishio's theorem.

A defense of Marx's original analysis can be found in Yaffe (1973).

Rosdolsky (1977, chap. 26) gives a careful and thoughtful analysis of the relation of the tendency for the rate of profit to fall to the other important ideas in Marx's work.

A thorough summary of empirical evidence on the rate of profit has been written by Dumenil, Glick and Rangel (1984a, 1984b), who also give references to the existing empirical literature on this problem. See also Weisskopf (1979, 1981) and Munley (1981) for their estimates of the movement of the rate of profit.

9. The Theory of Capitalist Crisis

The empirical facts about business cycles that have been established by observation are well summarized in Moore (1983) and Zarnowitz (1985). The latter also gives a very complete bibliography of work in this field.

There are two particularly finished passages in Marx's own work dealing with crisis in *Capital* (3.15.3) and in *Theories of Surplus Value* (1963, pt. 2, chap. 17).

Sweezy (1949) and Shaikh (1978) give helpful summaries of the main issues involved in understanding Marx's views of capitalist crisis.

Foley (1986a) gives a more complete discussion of Marx's critique of Say's Law.

Other useful readings, for those who want to delve more deeply into these questions, are by Dobb (1940), Robinson (1960), Harris (1978), and Aglietta (1979).

10. Socialism

The most illuminating texts for the problem of Marx's conception of socialism come from the very beginning and the very end of his intensive concern with economics, the *Manifesto of the Communist Party* (Marx and Engels, 1848) and the *Critique of the Gotha Program* (Marx, 1875). The last pages of *Capital* (3.48–52) are an eloquent summary of his view of capitalism and his own critical work.

Lenin's *State and Revolution* (1917) is a very influential development of Marx's ideas about the practical emergence of socialist society.

Lukacs's *History and Class Consciousness* (1922) powerfully develops Marx's theme of the ways in which the commodity fetishism of capitalist society and the development of working class consciousness lead to revolutionary socialism.

References

Aglietta, M. 1979. *A theory of capitalist regulation*. London: New Left Books.

Althusser, L., and E. Balibar. 1970. *Reading "Capital."* London: New Left Books.

Avineri, S. 1968. *The social and political thought of Karl Marx*. Cambridge: Cambridge University Press.

Baumol, W. J. 1974. The transformation of values: what Marx "really" meant (an interpretation). *Journal of Economic Literature* 12:51–62.

Bortkiewicz, L. von. 1949. On the correction of Marx's fundamental theoretical construction in the third volume of *Capital*. In *Karl Marx and the close of his system*, ed. P. Sweezy. New York: Augustus M. Kelley.

Bowles, S. 1981. Technical change and the profit rate: a simple proof of the Okishio theorem. *Cambridge Journal of Economics* 5:183–186.

Braverman, H. 1974. *Labor and monopoly capital*. New York: Monthly Review Press.

Brunhoff, S. de. 1967. *Marx on money*. New York: Urizen.

Bukharin, N. 1972. *Imperialism and the accumulation of capital*. New York: Monthly Review Press.

Dobb, M. 1940. Economic crises. In *Political economy and capitalism*, ed. M. Dobb. London: Routledge and Kegan Paul.

Dumenil, G. 1980. *De la valeur aux prix de production*. Paris: Economica.

Dumenil, G., M. Glick, and J. Rangel. 1984a. The tendency for the rate of profit to fall in the United States, Part 1. *Contemporary Marxism* 9:148–164.

—— 1984b. La baisse de la rentabilité du capital aux États-Unis: inventaire de recherche et mise en perspective historique. *Observations et Diagnostiques Économiques* 6:69–92.

Economic Report of the President. 1984. Washington, D.C.: Government Printing Office.

Edwards, R. 1979. *Contested terrain*. New York: Basic Books.

Fine, B., and L. Harris. 1979. *Rereading "Capital."* New York: Columbia University Press.

Foley, D. 1982. The value of money, the value of labor power, and the Marxian transformation problem. *Review of Radical Political Economics* 14(2):37–47.

—— 1983a. On Marx's theory of money. *Social Concept* 1(1):5–19.

—— 1983b. Money and effective demand in Marx's scheme of expanded reproduction. In *Marxism, central planning, and the Soviet economy: essays in honor of Alexander Erlich*, ed. P. Desai. Cambridge: MIT Press.

—— 1986a. Say's law in Marx and Keynes. *Cahiers d'Economie Politique*, 10–11:183–194.

—— 1986b. *Money, accumulation and crisis.* New York: Harwood Academic.

Godelier, M. 1975. *Rationality and irrationality in economics.* New York: Monthly Review Press.

Harris, D. J. 1972. On Marx's scheme of reproduction and accumulation. *Journal of Political Economy* 80:505–522. (Also in Howard and King, 1976.)

—— 1978. *Capital accumulation and income distribution.* Stanford: Stanford University Press.

Hartman, H., and A. Markusen. 1980. Contemporary Marxist theory and practice: a feminist critique. *Review of Radical Political Economy* 12(2):87–93.

Hegel, G. W. F. 1830. *Hegel's logic: being part one of the "Encyclopedia of the Philosophical Sciences,"* tr. W. Wallace. Oxford: Clarendon, 1975.

Howard, M. C., and J. E. King, eds. 1976. *The economics of Marx.* Harmondsworth: Penguin.

Kalecki, M. 1943. Political aspects of full employment. In M. Kalecki, 1971, pp. 138–145.

—— 1971. *Selected essays on the dynamics of the capitalist economy.* Cambridge: Cambridge University Press.

Keynes, J. M. 1936. *The general theory of employment, interest, and money.* London: Macmillan.

Lenin, V. I. 1917. State and revolution. In *Collected Works.* Moscow: Foreign Languages Publishing House.

Levine, D. 1975. The theory of the growth of the capitalist economy. *Economic Development and Cultural Change* 23:47–74.

Lichtheim, G. 1964. *Marxism.* New York: Praeger.

Lipietz, A. 1982. The "so-called transformation problem" revisited. *Journal of Economic Theory* 26:59–88.

Lukacs, G. 1922. *History and class consciousness.* Reprint, tr. R. Livingstone. Cambridge: MIT Press, 1971.

Luxemburg, R. 1913. *The accumulation of capital.* Reprint. New York: Monthly Review Press, 1951.

Mandel, E. 1968. *Marxist economic theory.* New York: Monthly Review Press.

Marglin, S. 1974. What do bosses do? The origins and functions of hierarchy in capitalist production. Part 1. *Review of Radical Political Economics* 6:60–112.

—— 1975. What do bosses do? The origins and functions of hierarchy in capitalist production. Part 2. *Review of Radical Political Economics* 7:20–37.

Marx, K. 1859. *A contribution to the critique of political economy,* ed. M. Dobb. Reprint. New York: International Publishers, 1970.

—— 1867. *Capital: a critique of political economy.* Vol. 1, *The process of production of capital,* ed. F. Engels. Reprint. New York: International Publishers, 1967.

—— 1875. Critique of the Gotha programme. In K. Marx and F. Engels, *Selected Works.* New York: International Publishers, 1968.

—— 1893. *Capital: a critique of political economy.* Vol. 2, *The process of circulation of capital,* ed. F. Engels. Reprint. New York: International Publishers, 1967.

—— 1894. *Capital: a critique of political economy.* Vol. 3, *The process of capitalist production as a whole,* ed. F. Engels. Reprint. New York: International Publishers, 1967.

—— 1939. *Grundrisse: foundations of the critique of political economy (rough draft),* tr. M. Nicolaus. Harmondsworth: Penguin.

—— 1963. *Theories of surplus value,* ed. S. Ryazanskaya, tr. Emile Burns. Moscow: Progress Publishers.

Marx, K., and F. Engels. 1848. The manifesto of the Communist Party. In K. Marx and F. Engels, *Selected Works.* New York: International Publishers, 1968.

Medio, A. 1972. Profits and surplus-value: appearance and reality in capitalist production. In *A critique of economic theory,* ed. E. K. Hunt and J. G. Schwartz. Harmondsworth: Penguin.

Meek, R. L. 1976. The falling rate of profit. In *The economics of Marx,* ed. M. C. Howard and J. E. King. Harmondsworth: Penguin, pp. 203–218.

—— 1956. *Studies in the labor theory of value.* New York: Monthly Review Press.

Moore, G. 1983. *Business cycles, inflation and forecasting.* Cambridge: Ballinger (NBER).

Morishima, M. 1973. *Marx's economics: a dual theory of value and growth.* New York: Cambridge University Press.

Munley, F. 1981. Wages, salaries and the profit share: a reassessment of the evidence. *Cambridge Journal of Economics* 5:159–173.

Okishio, N. 1961. Technical change and the rate of profit. *Kobe University Economic Review* 7:86–99.

Parijs, P. van. 1980. The falling-rate-of-profit theory of crisis: a rational reconstruction by way of obituary. *Review of Radical Political Economics* 12(1):1–16.

Ricardo, D. 1817. *The principles of political economy and taxation.* Reprint. New York: E. P. Dutton, 1973.

Robinson, J. 1960. *An essay on Marxian economics.* London: Macmillan.

Roemer, J. 1977. Technical change and the "tendency of the rate of profit to fall." *Journal of Economic Theory* 16:403–424.

Rosdolsky, R. 1977. *The making of Marx's "Capital."* London: Pluto Press.

Rubin, I. I. 1972. *Essays on Marx's economic theory.* Detroit: Black & Red.

Samuelson, P. 1971. Understanding the Marxian notion of exploitation: a summary of the so-called transformation problem between Marxian values and competitive prices. *Journal of Economic Literature* 9:399–431.

Schumpeter, J. A. 1939. *Business cycles: a theoretical, historical, and statistical analysis of the capitalist process.* New York and London: McGraw-Hill.

Sen, G. 1980. The sexual division of labor and the working class family. *Review of Radical Political Economics* 12(2):76–86.

Seton, F. 1957. The transformation problem. *Review of Economic Studies* 24:149–160.

Shaikh, A. 1977. Marx's theory of value and the transformation problem. In *The subtle anatomy of capitalism*, ed. J. Schwartz. Santa Monica: Goodyear.

—— 1978. An introduction to the history of crisis theories. In *U.S. capitalism in crisis*. New York: Union of Radical Political Economics, pp. 219–240.

Smith, A. 1776. *The wealth of nations*, ed. E. Cannan. Reprint. New York: Random House Modern Library, 1937.

Sraffa, P. 1960. *The production of commodities by means of commodities*. Cambridge: Cambridge University Press.

Steedman, I. 1977. *Marx after Sraffa*. London: New Left Books.

Steindl, J. 1952. *Maturity and stagnation in American capitalism*. New York: Monthly Review Press.

Sweezy, P. 1949. *The theory of capitalist development*. New York: Monthly Review Press.

U.S. Bureau of the Census. 1974. *Annual survey of manufactures*. Washington, D.C.: Government Printing Office.

Uno, K. 1980. *Principles of political economy*. Sussex: Harvester.

Weisskopf, T. 1979. Marxian crisis theory and the rate of profit in the post war U.S. economy. *Cambridge Journal of Economics* 3:341–378.

—— 1981. Rejoinder. *Cambridge Journal of Economics* 5:175–182.

Wolff, E. 1986. *Growth, accumulation, and unproductive activity: an analysis of the post-war U.S. economy*. New York: Cambridge University Press.

Yaffe, D. S. 1973. The Marxian theory of crisis, capital, and the state. *Economy and Society* 2(2):186–232.

Zarnowitz, V. 1985. Recent work on business cycles in historical perspective. *Journal of Economic Literature* 23:532–580.

Index